values
& ethics

can I make a difference?

values

& ethics

can I make a difference?

**Tony Fahey • Lorna Gold • Bishop Willie Walsh
Robert Putnam • John Quinn • Gerard Hartmann
John Abbott • Peter Abbott**

Edited by Harry Bohan and Gerard Kennedy

CÉIFIN

VERITAS

First published 2003 by
Veritas Publications
7/8 Lower Abbey Street
Dublin 1
Ireland

Email publications@veritas.ie
Website www.veritas.ie

ISBN 1 85390 658 1

A catalogue record for this book is available from the British Library.

Cover design by Colette Dower
Printed in the Republic of Ireland by Betaprint Ltd, Dublin

CONTENTS

CONTRIBUTORS

John Abbott is President of the 21st Century Learning Initiative in the United Kingdom and the United States. Much of Mr Abbott's research explores new understandings about the human brain, intelligence and memory in order to better understand learning and how it can be further facilitated by schools and communities around the world.

Educated at St John's School, Leatherhead, and Trinity College, Dublin, he is a former high school geography and religious studies teacher and was one of the youngest headteachers in the UK when appointed to Alleyne's School, Stevenage, in 1974. Whilst headteacher, he introduced Britain's first fully computerised classroom. He is a fellow of the Royal Geographic Society.

John Abbott has been a consultant to the United Nations Development Programme, the United States Agency for International Development, and was invited by Mikhail Gorbachev to join the State of the World Forum. He has been keynote speaker at the prestigious North of England Education Conference, the Canadian Education Conference, and the USAID Annual Conference; as well as conferences in Australia, Japan, Malaysia, South Africa and South America.

Mr Abbott is married with three sons aged twenty-three, twenty and eighteen. He is also a master woodcarver.

Peter Abbott spent the first seventeen years of his life in Hitchin, Hertfordshire. In 1995 he moved with his family to Reston, Virginia, where he completed the final two years of high school. In 1997 he spent four months working for the Chief Deputy Whip of the Republican Party, J. Dennis Hastert, in Washington, DC. In 1998 he lived in London for six months, working for the Liberal Democrat's chief education spokesman, Don Foster MP.

In 1999 he returned to work for Hastert who by this time had become Speaker of the US House of Representatives. In October 1998 Peter matriculated at Magdalene College, Cambridge, graduating three years later with a double First in English Literature. Whilst at Cambridge, he wrote for *Varsity*, the student newspaper, and served in various positions at the renowned Cambridge Union Society. In 1999, whilst serving as the Society's Press Secretary, he organised a forum on the Kosovo war, bringing together for the first time representatives of the Kosovo Liberation Army and the Bosnian government. In Lent Term 2000 he was elected President of the Society.

He is currently working in Los Angeles for syndicated columnist, author and political pundit, Arianna Huffington. In October 2002 he hopes to return to Cambridge to study for a PhD in dramatic tragedy.

Fr Harry Bohan is a native of Feakle, County Clare. Following his ordination, he studied Sociology in the University of South Wales, Cardiff, where he received an MSc. Econ. He is recognised as one of the leading social commentators in Ireland during the past twenty-five years and has been the driving force behind several practical projects aimed at strengthening family and community, including the Rural Housing Programme. He instigated the 'Our Society in the New Millennium' series of national conferences, which have been held annual since 1998.

Dr Tony Fahey is a sociologist and Senior Research Officer in the Economic and Social Research Institute, Dublin. He has published extensively on the family, religion, demography, the elderly, housing, and various aspects of social policy. He is a member of the International Steering Committee of the European Values Study and with colleagues in Queen's University Belfast and University College Dublin was responsible for conducting the 1999-2000 round of the European Values Study in the Republic of Ireland and Northern Ireland. He is the lead author of a comparative study of values and attitudes in the Republic of Ireland and Northern Ireland which will be published in autumn 2002. With Brian Nolan, he has recently commenced a study on wealth and housing in Ireland and Europe based on relevant data from the European Community Household Panel Survey.

Dr Lorna Gold currently holds an ESRC research fellowship examining business/civil society responses to the adverse impacts of globalisation. In particular, her research to date has focused on the global Economy of Sharing Network – a radical business-civil society response to the inequalities of globalisation. She is part of the Development Studies Research Group in the Department of Politics, University of York. She was awarded her PhD in Human Geography, 'Making Space for Sharing in the Global Market', from Glasgow University in December 2000. The thesis is soon to be published by Ashgate in book form.

As well as her academic work, Lorna is an enthusiastic advocate of the values she believes in. She is on the directorate of New Humanity, an NGO working for greater international solidarity with special consultative status at UN ECO/SOC. Over the past year, she has been active in the preparations for the UN Conference on Finance for Development.

Gerard Hartmann is a native of Limerick City. An accomplished athlete in his day, Gerard won numerous underage titles at national level before embarking on an athletic scholarship to the University of Arkansas, USA, in 1979. In 1988 Gerard returned to the USA to pursue a career in sports medicine, studying at the University of Florida and at the Florida Institute of Natural Health, qualifying as a sports injury physical therapist.

Gerard has worked at three Olympic Games – as physical therapist to a dozen medal winners at the 1992 Barcelona Games, physiotherapist to the Irish Olympic team, Atlanta 1996, and physiotherapist to the Great Britain Olympic team, Sydney 2000. His client list includes some forty-nine Olympic medal winners and thirty-four world champions and world record holders.

Gerard's clinic, Hartmann International Sports Injury Clinic, originally based in Florida, has been situated in his native Limerick since 1997.

Robert Putnam is Malkin Professor of Public Policy at Harvard University. He is a member of the National Academy of Sciences, a Fellow of the British Academy, and President of the American Political Science Association. His books include *Bowling Alone: The Collapse and Revival of American Community* (2000), *Democracies in Flux: The Evolution of Social Capital in Contemporary Society* (2001), *Disaffected Democracies: What's Troubling the Trilateral Countries?* (2000), *Making Democracy Work: Civic Traditions in Modern Italy* (1993); and *Double-Edged Diplomacy: International Bargaining and Domestic Politics* (1993). He has taught at the University of Michigan and served on the staff of the National Security Council. He is currently working on a multi-year project to develop practical strategies for civic renewal in the United States.

John Quinn has been a senior producer with RTÉ Radio 1 since 1977. His programmes have won numerous distinctions, including three Jacobs Awards and International Awards in

Japan and New York. He specialises in educational series and documentaries. His weekly educational magazine *The Open Mind* is now in its fourteenth and final year. Born in Ballivor, Co. Meath, he was educated at Patrician College, Ballyfin, Co. Laois, and St Patrick's College of Education, Dublin. A former teacher at both primary and post-primary levels, he is a recognised editor in educational publishing. He has written five novels, four for children, one of which won a Bisto Children's Book of the Year Award, and has edited three best-selling publications from his radio programmes 'Portrait of An Artist as a Young Girl', 'My Education' and 'The Open Mind Guest Lectures 1989–1999. In January 2003 the University of Limerick will award him an Honorary Doctorate in Literature in recognition of his contribution to broadcasting and education over the past twenty-five years.

Bishop Willie Walsh is a native of Roscrea, Co. Tipperary. He was educated at Corville National School, Roscrea and St Flannan's College, Ennis. He studied for the priesthood at St Patrick's College, Maynooth, and the Irish College, Rome. He was ordained a priest in Rome in 1959. After ordination he completed his studies in Canon Law at the Lateran University in Rome. On his return to Ireland he taught for a year at Coláiste Einde, Galway, and joined the staff of St Flannan's College, Ennis, in 1963. In 1988 he was appointed curate at Ennis Cathedral and became administrator there in 1990. He has been pastorally involved with ACCORD (formerly the Catholic Marriage Advisory Council) since its foundation in the Killaloe diocese. He has worked with Marriage Tribunals at diocesan, regional and national levels. He has pursued a life-long interest in sport and has been involved in coaching hurling teams at college, club and county grades. He was ordained Bishop of Killaloe on 2 October 1994.

INTRODUCTION

Harry Bohan

The work of Céifin in the last few years has been an attempt to read the signs of our times and, especially, to listen carefully to the real concerns of people and to respond.

You could ask what can we, or anyone else, add to the torrent of words and ideas in circulation? We are, for sure, living through an extraordinary period in Irish society. In material terms, many of us never had it so good, and indeed a lot of people feel good about life in Ireland today. But there is no escaping the exposures, the tribunals and the scandals that have filled the papers and are taking up so much airtime both here in Ireland and elsewhere. They have alerted us to a serious ethical and moral problem in the worlds of business, politics and religion, but also in our everyday lives. Some people would even suggest we are living outside a moral/ethical framework. Many of us are confused, angry and cynical. We all know that whether it is at home or at school, at work or in our communities, we can only survive on the basis of trust, and yet, our society seems to be experiencing a fairly serious breach of trust. This leaves us with a huge challenge, not just to identify the key issues, but much more important, to work out together what we can do about restoring trust.

There is no need for me to dwell on these breaches of trust except to say that the scandals that have plagued modern Ireland with regularity in recent years are effectively the betrayal of the present generation by the preceding generation. They call attention to the civic nature of morality.

Our hope is that *Values & Ethics: Can I Make a Difference?* will help us to clarify some of the issues we need clarified, but also inspire us to take initiatives in our own life which will effectively rebuild trust between people. We can so easily live in the comfort of talking about somebody else's story or scandal, but do nothing ourselves. These issues have to be dealt with truthfully, openly and honestly. But we must not allow ourselves to be over cynical or feel too helpless. We need to move on. And my hope is that *Values & Ethics* will give people a determination to do just that.

We all have to live our lives and there is every indication that the reconstruction of society will take place where people are. If all politics or religion is local, certainly relationships and connections are very local. They are best developed where life is lived. There is every indication that the twentieth century was the era of the organisation man and woman. Institutions wrote the script for us. They are now faced with the challenge of re-form and re-connecting to the lived experience of people.

In our world today we have all kinds of rights – the right to information, the right to access, the right to know what is going on – but there are other rights. Children have the right to innocence. Young people have the right to grow up and we all have the right to trust.

And so I think this is an appropriate time for people from a cross section of Irish society to come together to debate the place of values and ethics in our society and what difference each one of us can make. And we have a right, too, to demand good leadership. We have a right to look for leaders with two basic qualities – character and competence.

A good leader creates a vision that others can believe in and build together. And a good leader always acts honestly. Year after year in almost every study, people rank honesty as the single most important quality in a leader – be they parent, or politician, or teacher, or bishop, or corporate executive. In all my life I have seen again and again that people will accept almost any hardship or bad news if they know you are being straight with them. I also feel that people are much angrier with leaders who are not straight with them than with the wrong itself.

The second area we need to tackle is a much deeper problem and this is a crisis in personal moral character at grassroots level. It was once said that: 'A man cannot govern a nation if he cannot govern a city; he cannot govern a city if he cannot govern a family; he cannot govern a family unless he can govern himself; and he cannot govern himself unless he is subject to the needs of others.'

And so *Values & Ethics* tries to underline that we need to identify what really matters to us, what are our personal values, what are the things which make sense out of life. Every part of *Values & Ethics* deals with different aspects of values-led-living – things like:

- truth and honesty
- human life itself
- connecting with ourselves, the inner dimension of life
- connecting with others

In *Values & Ethics*, Gerard Hartmann looks at why we need champions – champions at all levels of society – to raise us up, to indicate to us what can be done, and to underline the importance of reaching out to others. We also look at the values across the generations with Dr Tony Fahey; Dr Lorna Gold looks at how the world of business can relate to the human dimension of life; Bishop Willie Walsh discusses the importance of valuing principles above privileges; and Professor Robert Putnam looks at the need to invest time and effort in rebuilding social trust and connections between people in communities. We reflect on a framework for a new reality with inputs from John Abbott and his son Peter.

I think we will all agree that this is an appropriate time for debate on values and ethics and my hope is that each one of us will be reminded that the people in our communities are alive, that despite the great differences that might sometimes separate us, we still form a community, share a tradition and beliefs, ancestors, misfortunes and joys.

They are the people we walk the journey of life with and their story is important.

On behalf of Céifin, I offer my congratulations to Dr Mary Redmond, the recipient of the 2002 Céifin Values-Led Change Award. This award is merited for her work on behalf of the Irish Hospice Foundation of which she is a founder member and in recognition of all the people who have contributed so much to the development of the Irish Hospice Movement over many years.

My thanks to Gerard Hartmann for delivering the opening address and getting us off to a terrific start. We are very grateful to our speakers and chairpeople for giving their time so generously and for their excellent presentations and thorough preparations.

A new feature of this year's conference has been the workshops on 'Values in Practice', which proved very successful. I would like to thank the following people who prepared presentations: Cllr Patricia McCarthy, Member of Shannon Town and Clare County Council; Ms Bernadette Phillips, Co-ordinator, Waterford Student Mothers Group; Dr Eamon Conway, Head of Department, Theology & Religious Studies, Mary Immaculate College; Mr Breandan O'Broin, Director, Creative Planning, Leo Burnett Associates; Mr Liam Moggan, Facilitator, Centre of Excellence, University of

Limerick; Ms Ann Dolan, Lecturer, Mary Immaculate College; Mr Des Ryan, H.R. Manager, Roche (Ireland) Ltd. I want to extend a special thanks to Martin Kennedy who facilitated the half-day and contributed to the overall success of the workshops.

On a final note, I want to thank Dr Kate Ó Dubhchair for her wonderful support and contribution towards the development of Céifin. We are sorry to lose her and wish her every success in her future career.

This conference would not be possible without the support of our sponsors. I sincerely thank the ESB, Waterford Crystal, West County Hotel and Gilbeys. I would also like to thank the Céifin staff, RRD staff and all our volunteers for their hard work and commitment to making this conference a huge success.

Harry Bohan
January 2003

WHY DO WE NEED CHAMPIONS?

Gerard Hartmann

I returned from the USA to live in Ireland in 1998, at the height of the Celtic Tiger. I was shocked and upset to see such a huge spiritual vacuum in the minds and hearts of so many young people, a huge loss of faith, a huge loss of vision, a huge loss of hope, a huge loss of values and a loss of ideals. It saddens me to see so many young people dependent on alcohol and drugs to seek pleasure and to escape from problems. So many young people experiencing a lack of purpose in life.

As their faith diminishes and training in self-denial and discipline disappears young people are looking for instant gratification and the short-term pleasures that drink and drugs provide.

So many young people experiment with drugs out of curiosity, peer pressure, or the desire to escape from pain and depression. Some youngsters I spoke to in Limerick explained that they use drugs to cope with the stresses of today's world. They claim to experience a lack of meaning and purpose in life. So many begin by experimenting and then go on to become dependent. We all must work together to make a difference.

Children must be educated and trained to deny themselves, to discipline themselves, to put off pleasures. If they are not given a spiritual view and hope for life beyond this world, then the young are candidates for getting hooked on self-destructive habits – the excessive consumption of food, smoking, the consumption and abuse of alcohol and drugs.

As a physical therapist, I specialise in treating the injuries of world-class athletes and preparing them, both physically and psychologically, for the rigours of competition at world class and Olympic level. I strongly believe that sport and recreation are the alternatives, the way forward, they are the way out of today's drink and drug culture.

I was born in Limerick in 1961, the eldest, and only boy, in a family of four. My parents, Paddy and Thecla, have been wonderful. They have supported me, loved me, trusted me, believed in me and – more importantly – they gave me the gift of faith, which as I grow older I value more and more. My mother's motto has always been: 'The family that prays together stays together'. As a young boy, I often looked up to heaven in despair when the rosary beads were taken out in the evening and study time or an all-important TV programme was disturbed for family prayer. It is only now that I am grateful for having being reared in a secure Christian environment of love, faith and understanding.

In my youth, parents were the main influence in a child's life; their influence was often backed up by the values of the school, Church, neighbours, relatives and friends. Today's youth are torn between contrasting and conflicting values and truths. The influence of the media is enormous and probably constitutes the greatest single challenge that parents face. The influence of the media on family life is diametrically opposed to traditional family values of stability, interdependence and fidelity. Parents have an enormous responsibility to maintain a strong family relationship. Children growing up in a loving, supportive family have the best chance of becoming responsible caring adults. Equally a child who is unjustly criticised or deprived is more likely to have difficulties.

When I was eleven years of age I was very tall for my age. Any parent whose child is either too tall, too small, too thin, or too fat knows that bullying is a likely consequence. At school boys from classes two and three years ahead of me were always setting up the toughies of their class to take me on in fist fights. During recreation times I often hid in the toilets or at the back of the school for fear of being forced into yet another fight. Those early days were trying in other ways. Rugby was the only sport and it was very competitive. You either made the grade or were left on the sidelines. I was too awkward and clumsy at that age so I had an immediate dislike for sport.

A wine gum was to signal the end of my schooling at that school.

One afternoon, minutes after settling back to class after lunch break my schoolmate at the desk beside me passed over a wine gum. Seconds later Fr Hugh called from the front of the class room 'Gerry Hartmann, are you chewing gum?' Caught in the act, and after one big gulp, my answer was 'No Father'. I was called to the front of the classroom in front of twenty-eight students. Fr Hugh reached into his cassock, withdrew a long leather strap and slapped it across both sides of my face. Without thinking I kicked him on the shin. I was immediately suspended and never set foot inside that school again.

I only tell this story to express how environmental conditioning affects us both positively and negatively. I believe we are all born to be positive and conditioned to be negative. We all need encouragement. If we mix with people who are positive, cheerful, enthusiastic and expecting the best, if we are lucky to have teachers who are supportive encouraging and fair, then we have a good chance of being positive, cheerful and successful.

I underwent my secondary schooling at Salesina College, Pallaskenry, County Limerick. To this day I am thankful to the Salesian order. Education was never forced, all pupils whether athletic or not were encouraged to participate in sport for enjoyment.

I will always remember a quote from St John Bosco, founder of the Salesian order, 'The teacher who is seen only in the classroom, and nowhere else, is a teacher and nothing more; but let him go with his boys to recreation and he becomes a brother'. At the Salesian College students were encouraged to try various sports; I remember participating in football, hurling, and basketball and while I never made a school team I had fun. In my second year I won the school league in table tennis and when the school sports were being held in May students were encouraged to participate in one of the many events.

Fr Martin Loftus was the sports master and he obviously recognised my athletic talent as he encouraged me to run and he organised a group of students to participate in the Munster schools athletics.

I won many Munster and all-Ireland underage titles and two months after my leaving certificate exams in 1979 I was away to the States on an athletic scholarship to the University of Arkansas. In 1978, when I was in fifth year, I saw a documentary on the starving people of Africa, so I did a fundraising run of twenty-five miles, running from Palaskenry into Limerick city and back to help them. I was sixteen years old at the time and the impact of seeing so many people starving and suffering inspired me to do something to help.

My experience in the contrast of treatment in the two schools I attended always impresses upon me the fact that everyone has a talent. It just takes the right support and encouragement to find and nurture it.

In the USA I studied Business Administration and pursued my athletic career. Sport gave me a chance to see the world and to meet people from different cultures and nationalities. I returned to Ireland in 1983, and in 1984 won the first of seven national triathlon titles and Iron Man events.

In 1986 a chance meeting with a old friend was to change my life. He had beaten me many times in running races. It had been seven years since our last meeting. He was overweight now and he explained that he regretted not pursuing his athletic dreams. In 1980, when he was offered an athletic scholarship, his parents sat him down and persuaded him to stay at home. He followed his parents' desire and went straight into the family business. It was obvious he was not happy in himself. One year later, he took his own life. His sudden death plagued me for for a long time. Here was a young man who had more athletic talent than I, but lacked the courage to follow his dream.

I thought hard, I prayed hard, and within a year I was back in the States pursuing my own dream. I was studying physical therapy and looking forward to a professional career in sport.

Two years before my friend's death I had witnessed another friend drop to his death from a window on the fifth floor of a building. I was standing twenty feet away when he hit the street. I remember clearly. Looking up to where he had jumped from, the window was wide open. Moments later a window two floors lower opened and I saw his mother look down at her son on the pavement. Within a minute she was down on the street covering her son's dead body with a blanket.

Sadly, of the twenty-eight classmates of mine at primary school, three ended their own lives prematurely. I have known nine men who have taken their own lives.

Had they no hope, no vision, no purpose? Was their darkness so great they could not see the light? Was the burden of life, of self-imposed and external expectations too great? Were they confused by conflicting messages on values and truths? Were they not lucky enough to find their talent, their calling in life?

One can only feel for the pain that they and their families went through. It is a complex and perplexing subject, and I have no answers – only questions and recommendations.

In August 1991 I won my seventh national triathlon title. Four days later, while out on a bike ride in Florida, my competitive sports career was ended in one split second. I was travelling at thirty-two miles per hour when an animal hit my front wheel. I shattered my hip and underwent emergency reconstructive surgery. I lay in a hospital bed for nine days and spent fourteen weeks on crutches. Straightaway, I made a decision: 'I am down, but not out'. I made the decision to take the energy and enthusiasm I had as an athlete and channel it into becoming the best physical therapist in the world.

That first year after the accident was the toughest period in my life. In one tragic moment my identity as a person, as a world-class athlete, was taken from me. I had to re-establish my identity and get accustomed to getting out of bed every morning with a new focus, a new goal. All through this difficult time I had an inner belief that it was all part of God's plan.

One year later I was treating twelve Olympic medal winners at the 1992 Barcelona Olympic Games. I have never looked back. Even through adversity, being positive, having faith and trusting in God is the only way I know.

I have served at three Olympic Games, with US athletes in Barcelona in 1992, as a physical therapist to the Irish Olympic team in 1996 and as physical therapist to the Great Britain Olympic team in Sydney 2000.

I am often asked what are the qualities that make successful sports people.

I would say that many, many sports champions have desire, passion, perseverance and an enthusiasm for what they do. They set goals and have a plan and, most important of all, they are positive and they believe in themselves.

Time and time again I hear people say, 'He or she is lucky to be such a great athlete.' Yes, we all need some luck, but investigate any successful person and you will find that hard work, preparation, dedication, commitment and a good support structure are at the core of this luck. The great golfer Gary Player once said, 'The harder I work, the luckier I get.'

Many youngsters are what I call 'late bloomers'. In sports terms they don't appear to have any talent; my next story is about a friend, a 'late bloomer', who went on to achieve international success.

Marcus O'Sullivan was a small lad from Cork who showed up to all the races. He was in my age category in juvenile competition, but he always finished well down the field. He was too small, he had no speed and we all felt bad for him because he tried so hard, but ended up outside the medals every time.

In 1979 at the Munster Championships I won the 800m, the 1500m steeplechase and the 3000m; Marcus had his best run ever, finishing second in the 3000m.

Afterwards he chatted to me about how he envied me getting an athletic scholarship, but his times were too slow to be considered. Marcus worked in a factory in Cork earning thirty pounds a week and continued to run.

No-one predicted that he would make it, but a year later, at nineteen, he made a breakthrough and won a scholarship to the famous Villanova University to be coached by Jumbo Elliott who was known as the 'masters of milers, maker of men', a man who coached many greats including Ronnie Delaney, Eamonn Coghlan and Noel Carroll.

Marcus is living proof that we should never underestimate anyone who has passion and takes something seriously. He persevered and, as his body matured, he developed his speed; the young boy who was too slow, who we felt bad for, went on to set national records at 800m. He competed in four Olympic games at 1500m and his achievement in winning three world indoor titles at 1500m is a record. He is the first to admit that he was never academically inclined, but when he got to Villanova he applied himself to his sport and study. The memories of working long shifts on the factory floor in Cork were all the encouragement he needed. He went on to receive a Master's in Business Administration from Villanova University and is presently the head track and field coach at Villanova.

Of all the great athletes I have had the pleasure to meet one man stands out – Kip Keino, father to my good friend Martin

Keino. He was the first Kenyan to make a major sporting impact, winning gold medals at 1500m and steeplechase at the 1968 Mexico Olympics. He is known as the father of Kenyan distance running. Kip grew up in the impoverished outskirts of Eldoret in a little village named Kipsamo. He was one of six children and was reared in a mud hut. No one could ever have imagined that a young boy from such a poor background would have such a humanitarian impact on the world.

The future was bleak in Kenya in the early sixties and the people lived either in extreme poverty or were lucky enough to be enlisted in the Kenyan armed forces or police force. When Kip joined the police at eighteen his life changed. He was introduced to competitive running and, with the success he achieved at Olympic level, he earned worldwide respect and, to this day, he is regarded as the greatest of all the Kenyan runners. The impact of his success spurred a running boom in his country and so many young boys and girls have followed in Kip's footsteps. They have seen that through running there is an opportunity and a way out of extreme poverty. In 1963 when Kip Keino was on police duty he stumbled upon two emaciated children. They had been abandoned. Their hunger was so great that they where eating dirt by the roadside. The local authorities gave Kip permission to care for the children and that was the start of his real calling from God.

Today, Kip and his wife Phyllis are parents to a hundred orphans. In the past thirty years they have reared over two thousand children. The two-hundred-acre farm 'Kuzi Mingi', which in Swahili means 'hard work', employs twenty-two staff. Kip and Phyllis take in babies who have literally been thrown away by their parents. Kip has rescued babies from public toilets, the roadside, and the bush. When I visited the orphanage Kip was proud to point out that from the thousands of orphans he has reared some have gone on to become doctors, nurses, university lecturers, or teachers, while others own their own businesses. They all received an upbringing, an education and a quality of life they would never have encountered without the Keinos.

Kip, who chairs the National Olympic Committee of Kenya, receives funding for the orphanage from the Kenyan Government and has used his world-wide contacts to gain support from the International Olympic Committee, Daimler-Chrysler, Oxfam and the Rotary Club.

Kip and Phyllis live modestly and work endless hours on an obvious mission from God. The Keinos have recently completed a school catering for eight hundred children. Kip takes great pleasure in repeating a little aphorism: 'We all came into the world with nothing and we shall leave everything here.'

Most people will know who Lance Armstrong is. He is a Texan who battled testicular cancer. He fought for his life. He regained his health against all the odds and returned to the sport he loved, cycling. Nobody gave him much of a chance of making it back to world-class level. Lance believed in himself and with his gritty determination he fought back. He has won the last four Tour de France titles, the most gruelling athletic events. His sporting success is a major victory for every cancer victim. Lance is their inspiration. He is their hero. He is proof that the battle must be fought and victory is attainable by those who have courage, the desire and faith to overcome adversity and illness.

In Ireland we had our own great cyclists. Stephen Roche and Sean Kelly dominated world cycling in the 1980s. Stephen Roche's cycling heroics put Ireland on the map.

In 1987 Stephen Roche went into the history books winning the Tour of Italy, the Tour de France and the World Championships in one season. He was the first ever sports person to be bestowed the highest honour in his home city when Dublin made him a Freeman of the City. Everywhere people warmed to Roche's performances and were cheered by his success.

Stephen Roche made a difference. Each one of you can make a difference.

Everyone can benefit from being involved in sport. Not everyone can be a champion at the highest level, but through sport each one of you can enjoy the freedom of movement, the exploration of your athletic talents, the emotions of winning and losing.

What Needs to be Done

I have spoken about the role models that have influenced and impressed me. We all need role models. We all need champions – heroes who can influence our lives and change our behaviour for the better.

I have outlined the positive and sustained influence of my parents, some of my teachers, of friends and of some of the sports people that I have been privileged to know and work with. They have helped to shape my life. They have helped me to form values, which in turn have helped me reach my dream. But where do the current generation look for role models?

We live in times of great change and many of the rocks of stability that existed when I was young have crumpled. What replaces them today?

The balance between what is positive and what is negative is often a delicate one. Ask any teacher or coach and they will tell you how easily the harmony, ethic and behaviour of a group can be altered. Many people will tell you how one incident or one supportive adult influenced them towards the positive.

Parents and families, volunteers in communities, coaches in clubs, teachers in schools, and local communities themselves all need support. They deserve your support. They need encouragement. They need recognition and gratitude for their efforts. Their role as a positive influence is needed more today that ever. You can provide a lot of that support.

My involvement in sport has changed my life for the better. I cannot imagine what my life would be like without sport. Many of the people who introduced me to sport, who motivated me, who gave up their time, and often their own money, have influenced me. Those people made a huge difference to me and I am very grateful. You can make a difference and influence someone for the better.

It should come as no surprise that one of my recommendations is that all youngsters should be given the opportunity to participate in sport. They should have easy access to facilities, good PE teachers and coaches, ample PE time in schools and competitive structures suitable to their age and ability.

In Kenya where Kip Keino has his orphanage, primary school students have PE every day. Why can't our children have PE in Primary School every day? The academic points race has reduced the impact of PE in many secondary schools and it has certainly reduced its importance in the eyes of many parents.

One downside to our technically advanced society is that not alone are many of today's youth unfit, but many are unhealthy. Due to an overabundance of food and a marked decrease in physical activity many kids are overweight. Being overweight or obese is linked to an increased risk of diabetes, heart disease, liver disease, some types of cancer, arthritis and other health problems.

'A healthy mind in a healthy body', was repeated many times in many circumstances when I was young. These days the importance of education through the physical has been eroded. Children no longer walk or cycle to school. They participate less in all forms of physical recreation. Physical Education in schools needs to be given a higher priority. Why not PE for every student, every day?

There are many reasons why children participate less in physical activity. Local facilities are not always available or accessible. The roads where my generation once played are now full of cars and unsafe. The local field has been developed. Housing estates without grass playing areas and without properly supervised indoor facilities have been allowed to spring up all over the country. Our local bodies have neglected the real needs of children.

Rather than spending exorbitant sums on a centralised National Stadium we should now, as a priority, develop the local structures first so that every child in every community can avail of their right of access to sport.

Sports clubs are now under enormous pressure because people are no longer as willing to devote time to club activities. Fewer people are willing to take responsibility for teams. Fewer people are willing to coach. The onus on the remainder is greater and greater. Adults themselves have less time and the ever-increasing demands of work, travel and other commitments mean that it is essential that volunteers are properly supported, encouraged and acknowledged for what they do.

Adults who devote their time to training and coaching teams and individuals should be supported and trained. The National Governing Bodies, many of whom are themselves supported by unpaid volunteers, need more support to develop participation and structures at grassroots level.

Such support at such a level is often hard to see. The world champion of tomorrow – the role model of the next generation – often only needs a field and a trained volunteer in order that he begin his journey to reach his or her potential. Michael Carruth became an Olympic Champion because his mother and father stood by his side and helped him through every stage. John Treacy became a two-time world champion and an Olympic silver medallist; he grew up and trained on the country roads of Villerstown, County Waterford. Sean Kelly's talent might never have been found had there not been a cycling club in Carrick-on-Suir.

Catriona McKiernan had no track, no multi-million euro stadium to train at. She prepared in the fields and on the perimeter of a golf course in Cornafeann in County Cavan. She had her brother, Peadar, and her coach, Joe Doonan, there through good times and bad. Today's child is tomorrow's champion.

Earlier I made reference to the human misery and destruction caused by the alcohol and drug culture. Young people need to realise that the short-term fix of immediate pleasure gained from drink and drugs will never replace the long term content and satisfaction of happiness. Pleasure is short term, happiness lasts. Through sport, young people can enjoy a healthy lifestyle, and go on to enjoy a healthy adulthood.

The young people are our future; they are the Ireland of tomorrow. They can be the champions – role models – if given the direction and opportunity.

VALUES IN A
CHANGING SOCIETY

VALUES ACROSS THE AGES

Tony Fahey

The following is a summary of a presentation to the Céifin conference delivered by Dr Tony Fahey of the Economic and Social Research Institute. The summary was prepared by the editors of this volume and omits the statistical tables and graphs included in the the original presentation.

In thinking about how to approach the issue of generational and age group differences and values systems in Ireland, it struck me that there is a line of commentary in this field that would be worth looking at. This line of commentary was exemplified in a piece in the *Irish Times* on 1 November 2002, which opened with the question: 'What is causing the decline in the quality of our life?' It went on: 'Few will disagree that while the quality of things we own has improved, our quality of life is declining', and followed this up with: 'The experience of being a young person in 2002 was one of loneliness, lack of purpose and engagement.'

By looking systematically at the evidence available in this field, I wish to decide if such a line of commentary is valid. Is it in fact true that, despite economic progress, people generally *feel* worse-off than they did before and think that, for all the material goods and money they now possess, they have lost something valuable from their lives? In answering this question, I want to look particularly at the young, because the commentary often focuses on their situation. I also intend to look at the situation in Ireland over the last two to three decades and make comparisons with what is going on in the rest of the world, particularly in Europe.

For this purpose, I will draw primarily on the 1999 European Values Study, which is a harmonised survey of a national, representative sample of adults, aged eighteen and over, in thirty-three European societies. The survey includes all of Western Europe and most of Eastern Europe. There were earlier rounds in 1981 and 1990 that were carried out in Western Europe only, as before the Berlin Wall came down Eastern Europe had not yet opened up to this kind of research. In addition, I will draw on Euro Barometer surveys that have been carried out in EU member states since the early seventies. In fact, Ireland has participated in and has been surveyed in the Euro Barometer Programme at least twice a year since 1973.

First, I am going to look at what some would call the 'feel-good factor' or, to put a more technical term on it, 'subjective well-being'. It is here that a lot of the negative commentary arises and people say, as the *Irish Times* said, 'We have more money but we feel worse' or 'Internally we feel that life is in decline.' The Euro Barometer surveys ask a number of questions about people's 'subjective states'. One of the most interesting versions of these is a question about life satisfaction – 'How satisfied are you with life these days?' Using five sample countries, I have examined the trends and responses to these questions over a thirty-year period. The Netherlands and Denmark have consistently emerged as having the highest levels of subjective well-being among EU countries. France and Italy have the lowest levels, and Ireland and Northern Ireland are somewhere in the middle.

In Ireland's case, one can see that there is a fairly steady decline in satisfaction levels in the responses to this question during the 1980s. The lowest level was reached in 1987. Since then there has been a pick-up and today the levels are more or less back to those of the 1970s. This would suggest that the 1980s were a particularly bad time in Irish life. Think back to the situation in Ireland at that time – crime was on the increase; drugs had begun to emerge as a serious problem, particularly in Dublin; unemployment had reached 17 or 18 per cent; emigration had returned and it looked like we were heading back to the situation of the 1950s. Suddenly in the early 1990s all of these problems began to be addressed to some degree at least and many of them, particularly on the unemployment front, were largely solved. In any event, however one might account for these trends in life satisfaction, they give no support to the idea that there has been a generalised decline in people's quality of life in recent decades.

So it seems clear when you look at responses to questions on life satisfaction across a wide diversity of societies that there is a very close relationship between the level of economic development in a country (as measured, for example, by GDP) and the mean level of satisfaction in that country. If we consider GDP per capita in thirty-three European societies in 1999, there is a cluster of countries, with Ireland more or less at the top, sharing high levels with Denmark, the Netherlands and a number of other countries. Western European countries cluster at very high levels of subjective well-being. The Southern European countries would be lower down on the scale – Spain, Portugal, and Greece. As you move into Eastern Europe you get extremely low levels of morale and subjective well-being. It is not that some people are very satisfied and that others are very dissatisfied in the Western European countries, it is rather that overall there is quite a high level of morale in the developed Western societies. As you go into the poorer societies of the world, it is not only that the mean level declines, but also the range of inequality widens. Inequality is measured by a statistic called Standard Deviation, which is a measure of how widely dispersed dissatisfaction levels are. As the mean level declines, that means that you get greater inequalities.

To give an illustration as to what this means, I have taken three sample countries, namely Ireland, which is one of the more satisfied or higher scoring on subjective well-being, Greece, which is in the middle, and Belarus, which is at the bottom. In the Irish case almost half the population score very highly on subjective well-being. Compare that with Greece where about a quarter of the population scores not so highly. Then we have Belarus: this is an example of a country with serious problems and serious quality of life, national morale and subjective well-being issues. Over half the population has scores in the lower section of the subjective well-being scale.

Looked at by age, there is no particular sign that life satisfaction in Ireland is particularly low for the young. There is a flat distribution across the age range. There isn't any great divergence by age. If you look at Western Europe in general that is also the case. There are somewhat lower overall levels, but no particular grade by age. In Eastern Europe you get a full gradient as age rises. It is the old who are particularly suffering in the poorer countries of Europe.

Another comment that is often made about Ireland is that the general public feels that public institutions have lost their authority and their appeal and that there is disenchantment and alienation as far as the public are concerned. Take a number of major institutions – Church, army, education system, the press, trade unions, police, parliament, civil service, and social welfare system. Respondents are asked to rate their satisfaction or confidence in each of these institutions. Putting all of them together they arrive at a composite score and compare that composite score across European communities. We see that Ireland has one of the highest levels of confidence in public institutions in Europe. I think it is useful to do this kind of thing. Whatever we may think about our problems, there are countries in the world that would love to have our problems because their situation both in subjective and objective terms is so much worse.

Malta, Finland, Ireland, Iceland and Denmark have very high levels of confidence in the public sphere, while Greece and some of the Eastern European countries have very low levels. Has the level of confidence in public institutions in Ireland, over time, risen or fallen? The Church is an important issue here. When the Church is included amongst the range of institutions to be measured, there has been a slight decline in public confidence between 1981 and 1999. If you look at the other institutions, leaving out the Church, then there has been a slight overall rise in public confidence in institutions. You may wonder how this can be in the light of all the scandals that have emerged in the nineties? Thinking back to the eighties, I can remember one of Gay Byrne's radio programmes where he announced to the nation that the country was 'banjaxed'. An air of despair was beginning to settle over the country, and this was reflected in the survey data collected in Ireland at the time. What has happened since? On one hand we have the stories about the tribunals and the scandals, but on the other hand there's more optimism in people's personal lives. For the first time ever people could grow up in this country without expecting to have to emigrate to find a job. For the first time ever there was full employment, people could switch jobs at will. This survey was taken in 1999/2000 when people could casually drop out of a job in the knowledge that they would get another. Living standards were rising very rapidly, so there were very positive things happening in people's own lives. The country was beginning to work in a way that it had not worked in the eighties. This is what is reflected in the confidence measurements.

Next, we break down and examine the individual public institutions and see which are rated highly and which are rated poorly in Ireland in 1999. The education system is a very highly regarded institution. The educational system is the sphere in public life with which the young have by far the most contact.

It is the most important influence on their lives outside of their own families. Also very highly rated in 1999/2000 are the Gardaí; traditionally, the Gardaí have always been very highly rated in Ireland. The Church used to be up at the same level, but it has dropped back. It is, however, still one of the more highly regarded institutions in Irish life. Andrew Greeley carried out a survey a couple of years ago that was a more detailed examination of this question, and he asked people to distinguish between their attitudes towards the hierarchy and towards their local parish clergy. Whereas the hierarchy was rated very poorly, the local parish clergy were generally rated very highly. They are two different dimensions of the same experience. One of those dimensions can be very positive even if the other dimension becomes very negative. Confidence in the Church in Ireland has declined from 51 per cent in 1981 to 22 per cent in 1999. On the other hand, if you look at the figures for 1999, 22 per cent have 'a great deal of confidence' and 32 per cent have 'quite a lot'. Put those together and that is 54 per cent who are still reasonably positive about the Church in Ireland in 1999. A lot of commentary is coming from the press. It is interesting to note that there is only one institution that ranks lower than the press and that's the Dáil!

Looking at the age issue, we ask: 'Is alienation from the public sphere happening among the young even if it isn't happening in society generally?' The results here do not particularly support the notion of an alienated youth. If you look at the education system as an area where the young have a lot of direct and practical experience, there isn't any great difference in confidence across the age ranges. In fact, over nearly a twenty-year period, from the early 1980s to the late 1990s, there is an indication of a steady increase in the positive attitude among the young towards the education system. Again I think the point might be raised that certain institutions have lost authority and lost respect among the young in Ireland, but some public institutions have gained in authority and in respect.

It often strikes me that one of the great achievements of the second half of the twentieth century in Ireland is the improvements that have occurred in the educational system. There is a very strong gradient by age in the Church's confidence ratings, showing that the young have become disaffected from the Church, but there are many other institutions where the young have a more positive or an equally positive view to their older counterparts. The European Union is one. Political parties generally have very low confidence ratings, but there isn't a particularly strong gradient by age. There is certainly nothing that compares with the age gradient for the Church. There is no consistent sign of alienation from the public sphere among the young.

Next we look at national pride; I have picked out the four years from 1982-1986 and 1997. First of all there is a general rise in the proportion of the population who say they are very proud to be Irish. Taking the youngest age group, in 1982, 48 per cent of 18-24 year olds said they were very proud to be Irish. By 1997, that had risen to 70 per cent. The sense of national pride has undoubtedly risen over the last two decades. On the issue of 'Very proud of own nationality in Europe' Ireland stands out. In fact, the level of attachment to Ireland as an entity is extremely high by European standards. There are other parts of the world – particularly the United States – that come in at similar levels, but the percentage of the population who are very proud of their nationality varies very dramatically across Europe. The Germans are at the bottom. That's the weight of their history, bearing down on their sense of nationhood.

Sense of control over one's life by age group is a general thing people are asked by the survey. 'On a scale from 1-10 how much freedom of choice and control do you feel you have over the way your life turns out?' Ireland has a particularly high positive response among the young. This does not seem consistent with the notion of the young being lost and aimless.

Let me turn very briefly to a third category, a third area of life. Some people refer to it as 'social capital' or 'simple social involvement'. Professor Robert Putnam in his book *Bowling Alone* has assembled statistics on trends of a very dramatic decline in this area in the United States; in the past we used to go bowling together and now if we go bowling at all, which we do less often, we are more likely to go alone. But does this apply generally across the Western world and, more particularly, does it arise in Ireland? One of the questions asked in the European Values Study is: 'How often do people meet with or spend time with friends or colleagues from work, from their church or clubs and voluntary associations?' The options are 'every week', 'once or twice a month', 'four times a year' or 'not at all'. When the results are put together to create an overall average for the population Ireland comes out at with a very high level of socialising by international standards.

On the issue 'Frequency in socialising by age group' we ask: 'Are the young all staying at home?' If you count going to Mass on a Sunday and include that in the average, it turns out that there is a very flat level of socialising across the ages. In other words there is no difference by age. If you exclude attendance at church you find that there is a higher level of social contact among the young than among older people. Whether this is unambiguously a good thing, that people are spending their time in pubs and getting drunk, is another question. Maybe there is a bad side to it, but it certainly means that the image of the isolated individual sitting at home watching television is not a particularly dominant feature of life in Ireland today.

Church attendance is a very important form of social contact, but weekly church attendance varies greatly depending on age group, social class and on whether the location is urban or rural. Only 27 per cent of 18-30 year olds claim to go to church every week compared with 89 per cent of those aged over 60. It is known from international research that people tend to overstate their level of church attendance, but even taking that into account there is a very strong age gradient here.

There has been a lot of talk about participation in voluntary organisations and very little hard evidence. The only evidence I could come up with was from two rounds of the European Values Study, 1990 and 1999. Two questions were asked: firstly, 'Do you participate in any of the following voluntary organisations?' There is a very long list and people say whether they participate or not. And secondly: 'Do you do any voluntary work for those organisations?' In 1990 49 per cent said that they were members that had risen to 57 per cent by 1999. The percentage who worked for at least one voluntary organisation was 27 per cent in 1990, and had risen to 33 per cent in 1999. I know that people who see these figures are quite surprised by them because the usual cry here is that it is very hard to get people to commit themselves to voluntary activity, but the number of voluntary organisations in Ireland over the years has simply exploded and one of the reasons that people find it so hard to man the voluntary organisations is that they are now in competition with more voluntary organisations than ever before.

I was quite amazed a number of years ago when we did some research on social conditions on local authority housing estates. One of the estates we visited was on the edge of Dundalk. It had its share of problems, but the local community development group there had just done an inventory of voluntary organisations in the estate and they came up with eighty-eight voluntary organisations. Even they were astonished by this. Most people in the area were aware of a few, but nobody was aware of them all. How an estate like that could sustain eighty-eight voluntary organisations is hard to credit, but nonetheless they were there.

I want to move on to try to draw some general conclusions. The first one is that the survey evidence simply does not support the theory of general negativism about trends in quality of life in

Ireland. It is certainly the case that material conditions have improved in many dimensions, and have consequently improved people's morale. We know from much of the research that one of the most damaging things to human morale, one of the most damaging forms of social isolation, is unemployment.

In the eighties, a large section of the population was affected by unemployment, or the threat of unemployment. By the nineties the unemployment problem was largely solved; we shouldn't be surprised that morale improved. Problems still exist, but they should be regarded as specific problems requiring specific targeted energetic solutions, rather than the more gloomy interpretation that they symbolise a general decay in the nature of social life. Those who suffer do exist. They are there, but they are not symptomatic of a general collapse. This only applies to countries that are really in serious difficulty, like some of those soon to be our partners in the European Union. It is only when you go there that you see the real level of demoralisation that can occur. We may well have had its parallel in Ireland back in the 1950s. The demoralisation that we had then is now largely gone. I often think, when we talk about the quality of life in rural Ireland in the past, of the fact that the West of Ireland stood out for having the highest rate of committal to mental hospitals ever on human record. It was the highest rate in the world at the time. People were shoved off into County Homes or shoved abroad. You can still see the legacies of 1950s Ireland on the streets of London and under the railway bridges of London. The homeless Irish account for a disproportionately large segment of the homeless population in Britain. So we comforted ourselves in the past that we had fewer problems than we did have by pushing them away, by shoving them under the carpet or by shoving them across the Irish Sea. I am not saying that all these problems have been solved, but we shouldn't be jumping to conclusions about overall downward trends.

There is no indication of particular problems among the young. The young always have problems. There are certain aspects of growing up that are inherently difficult. The young experience certain kinds of problems that pass once you settle down a little bit. It would be wrong to think that the youth in Ireland today are somehow in the grip of a malaise of a kind that has never been present before. If anything I would be inclined to think that the opposite is true. My own view is that one of the great advances in cultural life in Ireland in the last thirty years occurred with the introduction of the 1971 primary school curriculum. It was a major advance in educational philosophy. There have been a lot of failures in actually implementing it and there are a lot of schools and a lot of individuals for whom the educational system still does not work, but at least the ideals that lie behind the educational system have undoubtedly advanced. This is reflected in the attitudes of young people towards the educational system and the level of appreciation of the education system. Young people generally say they don't like going to school even now, as they did in my day, but they say it less vehemently now. I asked my own daughter how she felt about going back to school after her mid-term break and she said she was looking forward to it. I was astonished at that. I know nobody in my generation who ever had anything good to say about school. There are a lot of young people now who in their heart of hearts say: 'I really like school.' That, to my mind, is a very important advance, and one which we should be very conscious of.

In Ireland, there are no indications of a decline in social capital of the kind that Robert Putnam has identified in the United States. The post-war period in the United States was a golden age in American history, whilst in Ireland it was a crisis period. Ireland hit the floor in the 1950s and it would be scarcely surprising to find that things had picked up since then because they were so bad at the time that they could have hardly have got any worse. There has been a general improvement not only in the material side of life, but in most dimensions of social life as well. This is even taking into account the rising rate of crime, though with regard to rising crime rates, I would expect that if you were to quantify the history of interpersonal violence in Ireland it would show a less dramatic upward movement than people often assume. The level of violence that was practised with official sanction back in the fifties requires comparison. The most violent place I ever stood in was the primary school I went to. There was no attempt to control violence in that place and I know that in that same school now the ethos is completely different. The primary school that I went to was not a religious one. It was a standard, straightforward, national primary school. It was almost as if violence was applauded – spare the rod and spoil the child. Now the notion that children must suffer in order to develop into healthy adults has been completely turned on its head. It seems to me to be a major advance in the culture of Ireland and indeed in many other countries over the last thirty or forty years.

Irish people continue to be highly sociable and gregarious. Participation in voluntary organisations rose between 1990 and 1999. My own experience with voluntary organisations has been mostly with the GAA. I played juvenile football in County Meath and then drifted out of it as a seventeen- or eighteen-year old. I just came back to it four years ago when my eight-year-old son became interested in it. I live in Chapelizod in West County Dublin and the nearest GAA club is in Castleknock. I had lived in the area for ten or twelve years and had no knowledge of this club at all. It is one of the features of Dublin life that GAA clubs do not form the centre of the community the way they do down the country. I was astonished at how vibrant a club it is. There is something like thirty or forty teams fielded there every week. In fact, in Castleknock a couple of years ago a second GAA club was founded because they couldn't cope will all the numbers crowding into it. The most impressive thing about the GAA – having had no contact with them for twenty-five years – was the summer camp they ran.

The GAA were never renowned for their 'refinement', for want of a better word, but at the summer camp that I came across four years ago, they were highly organised and the attitude of care and respect that was there for the children was a truly impressive thing. It is to the great credit of the GAA that they can do that at ground level.

So overall the national mood is positive. People think this is a very provocative thing to say. I find that extraordinary! The national mood has been buoyed up by the recent economic progress, social attachment is strong, and optimism is rampant among young people, possibly more than it ever was in the past.

What does all this mean for Céifin and the Céifin Conference? Usually we are looking at social problems, but, for a change, it is worth looking at the overall picture and asking: 'Is the negativism validated by the evidence, such that we can assemble?' I think that there are two things about that negativism to bear in mind. One is that it undermines credibility. Those who wish to promote values must be able to recognise value where it already exists. We shouldn't damn a whole system because it isn't Utopia. It seems to me that one of the greatest difficulties the Catholic Church has in Ireland is its extraordinary inability to acknowledge good that has not emerged from within itself. A lot of the good that has emerged in the modern world, including the education system, has been imposed on Catholic culture from outside rather than being generated from within. The whole philosophy of childhood and how to treat children did not emerge from within the Catholic tradition. The Catholic Church is often extremely unwilling to acknowledge where cultural and moral progress takes place if they haven't created it themselves. Anybody who says: 'I am promoting values, but I do not recognise your values, I deny that you have a capacity to generate values if I didn't think of them first', is undermining their own credibility. The second thing is that it undermines effectiveness. The overly gloomy diagnosis distracts attention from the very many specific problems that require specific solutions. It sometimes occurs to me that if you went into a doctor and said 'Doctor I have a headache and I am not sure what is wrong with me' and he looked at you and said, 'God your suit is a mess, your teeth are bad, you are overweight, and you have a bad haircut' it wouldn't be the basis from which to start addressing the problem of your headache. If we start with a cataloguing of the failures that are there it becomes much more difficult to draw on the strengths in order to solve the problem.

'HUMANISING' THE GLOBAL ECONOMY

BUSINESS AND CIVIL SOCIETY IN PARTNERSHIP AS AGENTS FOR CHANGE

Lorna Gold

Introduction

In the past few years there has been plenty of rhetoric about 'humanising' the global economy. The phenomenon of globalisation seems to have polarised debates. Stereotypes are rife: on the one hand, there are greedy CEOs hell-bent on destroying the planet whilst lining their own pockets through corrupt dealings. Scandals such as that involving Enron have alerted us to serious ethical problems in the business community – an economic system that is so greedy that it now risks imploding on itself. On the other hand, who can forget the images of violence at Genoa, Gothenburg and Seattle? Anti-globalisation mobs dead set on stopping progress, causing havoc and destroying business. The message seems to be loud and clear: either you are for globalisation or against it.

- Taken at face value, there appears to be little middle ground and little space for real dialogue. For those who are anti-capitalist or anti-globalisation, all business is bad and, hence, the enemy. For those who believe in the primacy of the market freedom, all those who advocate a different approach are harking back to an era of inefficient intervention in the economy. This is, however, only part of the picture and skews the issues at stake in this important debate. Between these two extremes – of greed and violent reaction – there are many possibilities and many alternatives. Perhaps the most important thing we have to do is to find out where these are emerging and learn from the positive examples of change.

Setting the Scene

Most people tuned into the goings on in Johannesburg for the World Summit on Sustainable Development (WSSD) in 2002. We all saw the thousands of delegates and experts coming together and attempting to address some of the the critical problems facing our world today: chronic poverty, growing insecurity, environmental destruction, and so on. They are issues all of us know all too well, but perhaps it is worth just taking a moment to focus our minds on the scale of some of these problems.

Chronic Poverty and Inequality
- After half a century of uneven, but often rapid and widespread economic growth, the world is richer than ever before and has unprecedented technological capacity
- Whilst major improvements have been made in some aspects of well being – for example, infant mortality rates have fallen, access to basic education has improved – over half of humankind lives on less than two dollars a day, in or close to chronic poverty, and suffering severe deprivation of many kinds. Over thirteen million people in sub-Saharan Africa are currently facing starvation.
- Inequality of income, wealth, power and assets is growing between and within most countries. One simple statistic is enough to illustrate this: the 20 per cent of people with the highest incomes receive 86 per cent of global income.

Human Insecurity
- Whilst it is difficult to draw a straight line between poverty and global security problems, common sense tells us that a world in which there is increasing inequality – and

increasing communication of that injustice – will be a world of anger, hatred and violent reprisal. Such claims are backed up by a growing number of studies linking the need to rethink 'development' in terms of 'global governance'.

- The current neo-liberal model – *market freedom no matter what* – is acting as a smoke screen for international criminal groups. The liberalisation of trade, finance and investment – the main policy underpinning globalisation – has allowed the rapid economic growth of many countries, but it has also played a major role in facilitating the spread of criminal groups with ties to terrorism, drug dealing and arms. The deregulation of the arms trade, moreover, which has put economic considerations above all others, has enabled non-state actors to gain easy access to arms.

Environmental Destruction
- The complex environmental issues discussed at the WSSD ranged from global warming and fossil fuels to the destruction of bio-diversity, the depleting fish supplies, as well as air, water and land pollution. Suffice to say that at the heart of all these issues is an understanding of economic action devoid of any sense of responsibility both to future generations and to the planet. The concept of sustainable development rests on our capacity to integrate ethical concerns within our economic decision making.

All of us who followed these proceedings were dismayed – if not incensed – by the failure of the WSSD to address key concerns that will not only determine the futures of millions of people in dire poverty, but the future of our planet. The ostentatious surroundings and petty bickering of the discussions inside the conference were thrown into sharp relief by the reality of poverty and injustice just outside the door. Whilst many of the governments may have good ideas, and each individual may have strong values, somehow the sum of their efforts did not add up. The final outcome was almost inevitably a watered down compromise with no real substance for change.

From my own personal involvement in such negotiations, I can relate to that overwhelming feeling of helplessness. Three weeks after September 11th 2001 I found myself in New York at the preparations for the UN conference on Financing for Development. Expectations were high – amongst both delegates and NGOs. There was a general feeling that the tragedy of September 11th would lead to a new vision in international politics. The backdrop of suffering and grief seemed to permit us to glimpse a different kind of world in which compassion and co-operation had a role to play. In fact, the draft documents for this conference read like a wish list for all those who had been campaigning for years for positive change. Talking to delegates informally, one got the feeling that we were on the brink of something new – but each country was waiting for the other to take the lead. No-one wanted to be the first to break ranks, above all, with the US vision. In the end, the result was a rather watered down compromise with no real change in policy. Such experiences can leave you with a heavy heart.

One of the critical factors in this, and many other similar massive political failures, is that the underlying 'neo-liberal model' has come to dominate the circles making decisions not only in the economic, but also in the political fields. In the absence of shared beliefs and values across the world, neo-liberal globalisation has become a *de facto* ethic – a set of governing assumptions and values – in which the market decides who is valuable, and who is worthless; and the accident of birth ultimately decides who survives. As President Umbeki of South Africa said in his opening address to the WSSD, we are faced with a choice between 'economic Darwinism' or a new vision. But the vocabulary of change which could lead to that new vision seems to have slipped from the minds, if not the hearts, of those who make key decisions. But can we really throw up our hands and say that nature is taking its course in our economy? Can we really afford to let what has been called a 'technocratic autocracy' govern our world? In the name of economic freedom, it seems that everything we love and value can be eroded – from our more tangible assets such as the environment, to those assets which underpin the very fabric of human society – a sense of justice, respect for each other, capacity to care and share, ability to dialogue, to welcome those who are different – what I imagine Professor Robert Putnam would call 'social capital'.

Whilst there are many positive aspects of the global economic model today, and my plan here is not to offer some grand alternative, we have to face up to the negative consequences all around us – as illustrated above. These are not 'market imperfections', but the impact of a distorted understanding of what self-interest can achieve and blindness to the negative impact of self-interest on social foundations of society. They force us to re-think urgently how our economy relates to other aspects of life, in particular our ethics. The imperative of rethinking this model at a global level has accelerated since September 11th. Human security, and hence the very environment in which a free market can operate, is drastically undermined by current thinking. After all, an increasingly insecure and unpredictable world is in no-ones interest – neither business, citizens, or states. All of us have to work together to reshape it.

What does it mean to 'humanise' the global economy?
To get beyond the rhetoric of humanising the global economy, I would like to consider three arenas in which change can take place: in public policy-making, in private institutions and at a 'person-in-community' level. What are the key changes that need to take place in each sphere? How do they impact on each other?

Public Policy-Making
Firstly, change is needed at a public policy level, particularly in relation to global institutions. We need new models, new frameworks, fresh insights into economic, foreign and development policy. Recourse to bland ideological commitment to 'the market' or 'national interest' is no longer acceptable. The critical question today, as in 1980 when Willy Brandt wrote his famous report on the environment, is how we can reframe economic policies, in particular, in ways that enable us to think, not only about our own self-interest in the narrowest sense, but of *global self-interest*. In other words, our real domestic policy is global since we all share the one small planet. We can shuffle responsibility around it, but in the end none of us can get off it (though some billionaires are working on that one). This requires a radical change in perspective and an ability to think coherently about the overarching unifying vision in which all other policies have to be placed. In other words, it demands coherence. Many concrete and imaginative proposals that would strengthen this global vision are on the table, as mentioned before – such as setting policy in a human rights framework – but the will to move beyond political and economic expediency is sadly lacking.

Private Institutions
At the same time, humanising the global economy requires changes in private institutions. Most importantly, it requires a radical rethink of the role of business and civil society organisations. Despite the negative image and reputation that transnational business has gained over the past few years – and rightly so in many instances – much is being done to change this, as we will see further on. The rise of corporate social responsibility is symptomatic of much wider changes going on in the business community in their search for a new legitimacy. Moreover, on the part of civil society, there is more willingness to engage business in a positive agenda. The World Social

Forum – and the regional forums – are good examples of how change can be harnessed for good. Many have predicted that the future of business will lie not in its ability to oppose the mood of change, but in its capacity to harness the energy of the anti-globalisation movement and transform it into a positive agenda. Those who read the signs of the times carefully are already working on this.

Persons-in-Community

Finally, there is a need for change at the individual and community level. Each and every citizen needs to critically rethink how they make economic choices. We need to shift from life choices based solely on self-interest alone, to ones based on an ethic of responsibility – to our fellow human beings and the planet. Whilst in the past many of us may have begrudged the fact that there was no choice in such decisions, now we can *choose* to make a difference: supporting ethical investment, supporting micro-finance, buying fairly traded goods, taking an interest in how we impact on our environment. It means generating a new culture and becoming local agents of change in our communities.

So how do these three levels inter-link? The linkages between them are crucial. If we start from what is often seen as the 'top level', from policy, it is obvious that so long as political institutions govern on the assumption that people are out for themselves, no innovation that takes into account the needs of other countries or groups is possible. Realpolitik teaches that domestic concerns always come first. At a private institution level, moreover, if the widespread public perception is that competition is the sole governing principle – and that competition is based on price alone, regardless of the ethical implications of what is being done – then economic efficiency will take precedence over every other consideration. If individuals, increasingly devoid of a sense of community, believe that the world out there is a hostile jungle and that each person is out for themselves – from the politicians downwards – then the impulse to care for others and to care for the planet weakens. This universal belief in self-interest effectively locks people into a cycle of despair for the future.

Underpinning this is the need for a radically different vision to the dominant one today. It is a vision that no longer sees economic life as somehow detached from the rest of life, immune from the normal moral and ethical responsibilities that we face in our daily lives. It requires us to see economic space as a space which is relational – which involves myself and my relationship with others – be they near or far. It is an ethical space. Such an idea is not new – indeed it is one that has been around for many centuries in the texts of the world religions. It is a vision that is also summed up in the UN Declaration of Human Rights: 'Article 1: All human beings ... are endowed with reason and conscience and should act towards one another in a spirit of brotherhood ...'. In Article 28 it states that 'everyone is entitled to a social and international order in which the rights and freedoms set forth in this Declaration can be fully realized.' It is an explicit call to us to move beyond the rhetoric of neo-liberalism and actively foster international solidarity in view of development.

It is a view that many of us here may well share, but it is one that is seldom reflected in our economic choices. We may expect it to inform our personal dealings with others, but when it comes to economic action, we are taught from a young age that it is best to be out for number one. After all, if we add up the self-interest of everyone it will automatically become the self-interest of the majority. This seductive idea on which the current economic system is based is a fallacy. Even Adam Smith, that Scot who is often hailed as the Father of Economics, would turn in his grave at such an assertion. Whilst he recognised the role of self-interest, he spent most of his life as a moral philosopher, stressing the importance of other human values such as sympathy for others in living a good life.

One big problem at all levels is that we lack credible models to convince us otherwise. The model of 'the free market' is appealing in its simplicity. So where are these alternatives emerging?

Seeds of Positive Change: the Economy of Sharing

The examples of a different economy are all around us. Perhaps we are too scared to look – for fear that these new and emerging alternatives will challenge us and make us see that it is no longer feasible to say that there are no alternatives.

One positive example of where this is happening is a little known movement called the Economy of Sharing, which grew out of the Focolare Movement, an ecumenical movement committed to promoting unity and relationships based on mutual love and understanding at all levels. The Focolare Movement itself is a powerful example of how one person, motivated by a strong vision of humanity, can make a difference. The Focolare was started by one woman, Chiara Lubich, in the 1940s during the Second World War, and has spread across the world almost entirely through word of mouth, challenging individuals to change their hearts and commit themselves to becoming instigators of a *civilisation of love* wherever they find themselves. It is not some kind of esoteric, hippy love – but a solid love rooted in a practical and deep-rooted concern for fellow human beings, above all in the here and now. The heart of this movement, which now involves people from all the main world religions, is a return to the principle of the 'golden rule' found in many different religious traditions: 'Do to others as you would like them to do to you'. Simple as this may sound, it has given rise to a global community of several million people committed to putting this vision of unity into practice in their daily lives, with remarkable results. Each one of them, in their own way, has become a 'social innovator' committed to changing the lives of those around them through applying the values of trust, solidarity, co-operation and even love, to the communities in which they live and work.

One of the concrete results is the Economy of Sharing* that emerged in 1991 in Brazil and specifically concerns the small and medium business sector. Many individuals in the country were faced with the tragic effects of economic injustice every day. Unemployment, homelessness, poverty, crime – they witnessed the impact of what has been called 'unbridled capitalism', a phenomenon most clearly seen in the so-called developing countries where fragile social institutions are unable to resist the power of market forces. They decided to involve a small group of business people in applying their vision of unity into their organisations so as to create businesses that not only took from the community, but were designed to give back and to share with the poorest.

Since then, the EOS project has grown and now involves around eight hundred businesses in thirty-four countries throughout the world in advocating a new economy. It is still a minute number, but they are important examples of how the business community, motivated by a strong ethical vision, can respond to the imperative of humanising the global economy. They are spread across a wide range of sectors, including manufacturing and services.

Here are a few examples:
- In Brazil, there are now nine businesses in the Spartaco Business Park. The park was specifically set up as a pilot for the EOS and has become a focal point for academics and others interested in studying the nature of this economic phenomenon.
- Across the world a number of support businesses providing financial and technical back-up to the EOS network are emerging. In the financial sector, Solidar Capital is providing venture capital and support to new EOS businesses in developing countries.

- Ancilla Consulting has experienced remarkable growth as one of the leading consultancies in south east Asia. It bases its management training scheme around the seven principles of the EOS. These principles integrate the vision of unity into every aspect of corporate life.
- Many young people have taken up the challenge of the EOS, seeing business of this sort as a positive choice in making a difference in the world. One example of this is the 'Roberto Tassano Social Cooperatives Consortium' in Sestri Levante, Liguria. This consortium is now responsible for the management of a number of homes for the elderly, community homes for people with mental illness, and protective structures for people with special needs that are linked to industries in the local area. Over the past few years, the consortium has grown from a small initiative with a few founding members to eight hundred shareholders and has been defined as an 'enterprise incubator' due to its capacity to give rise to new productive activities.
- Here in Ireland, the successful language school, Language and Leisure International, came about as a consequence of the EOS and tries to apply the principles of the EOS in its everyday practice. The consequence is a dynamic business, but also an environment which is notable for the sense of welcome it gives to foreign students.
- The EOS has given rise to a movement involving business people, academics, policy makers and citizens from all over the world to build a new economy. They meet regularly to explore and deepen the vision that underpins the project, systematise the ideas underpinning it, and to look at ways of promoting an economy of solidarity.

The EOS can be seen alongside the numerous expressions of a new humanised economy which are emerging today. The businesses are committed, in every aspect of their activities, to putting the needs and aspirations of the human person, and the common good, at the centre of their attention. They operate within the market and to all intents and purposes are commercial firms like any other. At the same time, however, these businesses propose something different. For them, the true meaning of all their economic activities lies not in the economic transaction *per se*, but in making it a 'meeting place' or 'place of encounter' in the deepest sense of the word: a place of *communion*. A place of communion, therefore, between those who have economic means and those who have not; communion between all those who are engaged in the economic activity in different ways. Communion is a word seldom heard outside churches today, but it expresses clearly the vision of a humanised economy underpinning the EOS. If it is true that the economy itself often contributes to creating barriers between social classes and different interest groups, these businesses seek to be an antidote in several ways. Firstly, they set aside part of their profits to provide urgent help to those who are in difficult economic situations. Secondly, within the businesses, relationships based on openness and trust amongst all those with a stake in the business – consumers, competitors, local and international community, public administration – are promoted, always bearing in mind the wider interests of all. Finally, these businesses undertake to put into practice and spread a culture of *giving*, of *peace*, of *lawfulness* and of respect for the *environment* (recognising the need for solidarity with creation) both within and outside of the business. They share best practice and have developed their own guidelines as benchmarks.

So how can this individual and institutional change impact on policy? This apparently small, yet global project, is now indeed beginning to have an impact at an institutional and policy level. The witness of several hundred business people is being heard far beyond the reach of the individual businesses. Their perseverance, despite the difficulties of swimming upstream, is opening up the political space for an authentic dialogue, and the possibility of becoming authors of a new economy. At the very least, it is challenging the dominant vision of economic self-interest and offering insights into new ways of thinking and acting.

Conclusion: Rethinking Freedom

Exactly one year ago, I found myself staring into the chasm left by the destruction of the World Trade Center in New York. Looking into that void at the heart of the so called 'land of the free' made me realise that we urgently need to rethink our understanding of economic freedom. Our economic thinking has generally followed the *freedom from* perspective, seeing each individual as an isolated unit – free floating atoms competing for space. That vision, based on isolation, creates a paradox for human happiness, because one inevitably ends up building higher and higher walls to keep *the other* out. When that other is poor or destitute, desperation often results in violence. In the name of freedom, we end up turning our own homes and countries into self-made prisons. This vision is no longer tenable. We need a radical shift to a *freedom to* perspective – a vision that is much more challenging – since freedom to do things and to be somebody means taking relationships with others seriously in economic life. It means recognising that true freedom can never be obtained through isolation or self-interest, but through building relationships centred on solidarity, sharing and even love. No society, and certainly no economy, is capable of surviving without these values. Building bridges with others dramatically increases our freedom and potential to change, but also requires a capacity to feel empathy for our brothers and sisters. The experience of the EOS shows that this is possible, but it demands the courage to re-evaluate the ethics and values that we, as individuals, bring to our businesses, if we have one, and our lives in general. It means reorienting our vision to put *communion* at the heart of what we do. It is no longer feasible to leave our faith – whatever faith that may be – at the door of the office, like someone who hangs up their jacket. It means looking seriously at how our ethics and values relate to our work and guide our assumptions and practices. Once we make this important step, there are no limits to the difference each one of us can make.

IF WE VALUE PRIVILEGES ABOVE PRINCIPLES – DO WE LOSE BOTH?

Bishop Willie Walsh

A Soul for Ireland

It is over ten years ago – February 1992 – that Jacques Delors, then president of the EEC, gave his widely acclaimed talk entitled 'A Soul for Europe'. In that talk he argued that a successful Europe could not be built on what he called 'juridical astuteness and economic know-how'. 'If in ten years from now,' he said, 'we have not succeeded in giving a soul, a spirituality, a deeper meaning to Europe, we will have lost the game.'

Over ten years have passed. Because there is no system of goals and points to determine the outcome it is not clear whether Europe has lost the game or not. It is not clear whether Europe has found a soul, a spirituality, a deeper meaning. I do believe however that Delors plea for 'A Soul for Europe' needs to be matched right now with a plea for 'A Soul for Ireland'.

A Soul for a Bishop

I would understand if some people said that, of all people, a bishop has little right to speak of the need for a soul for Ireland at this time. One might even say he has a damn cheek to do so. The revelations of recent years have convinced many that the

Irish Church and in particular the Irish bishops have lost their soul. When I was asked in the first half of 2002 by the Céifin Committee to speak on the topic of privilege and principle, I had no inkling of the awfulness of what was soon going to come to light. The phrase 'had I known then what I know now' has been used and perhaps overused by both politicians and bishops in recent times. I am tempted to apply the same phrase to excuse my presence on the platform here this afternoon. I will resist the temptation however, because I believe that when one is pained and shamed and to some degree broken, then one is all the more open to searching for that lost soul.

In our search therefore for a soul for Ireland, a renewal of values and principles which might guide us in this twenty-first century, I would like to look in an orderly way at where we have come from, where we appear to be at the moment, and where we might begin to move from here.

Story of a Soul: Where We Have Come From?
Early Years
If we reflect briefly on the history of Ireland since independence it becomes very obvious that there were two dominant institutional forces, namely Church and State, which effectively determined much of the lives of the people. I believe that in the post independence years our politicians, the representatives of the State, were largely idealists who were prepared to work for the good of our people with little effort to count the cost to themselves. They appeared to be willing to serve without expectation of personal gain. The de Valeras and Cosgraves, the Lemasses and Costelloes, appeared to take for granted that their primary role was one of service rather than being served, one of principle rather than privilege.

The other dominant institution, the Church, was active in support of the State, building schools and hospitals and indeed operating these schools and hospitals largely on the basis of unpaid service of its own members. There was a vitality and a confidence in the Church which inspired so many young people to enter priesthood and religious life. They accompanied so many of our emigrants to the Anglo-Saxon world of Great Britain, United States and Australia, building the Catholic Church in these countries. Other priests and religious went to spread the good news of the Gospel in Africa and elsewhere.

There was, however, the darker side. The hand and glove operation of authorities of Church and State was often oppressive, authoritarian and without accountability in censorship laws and in ill treatment of those who somehow were unable to conform to the strict rules. This close connection sadly led to the Letterfracks and the Magdalen homes, of which those of us who lived in that time now feel a deep sense of shame. I had occasion to visit Letterfrack recently. Those of you who have some knowledge of that area will know what I mean when I say that, back in the 1940s, to send a boy from Dublin to Letterfrack, you might just as well have sent him, like the criminals of old, to Van Diemen's Land. And dare I say, it must equally have been Van Diemen's Land for many brothers sent there.

Dreams of the Sixties
Out of that censorious and repressive Ireland of the 40s and 50s we gradually moved to a time of new hope in the 1960s. Pope John XXIII opened the windows of the Vatican and called the Council known as Vatican II. Harold McMillan in his memorable phrase 'the winds of change are sweeping across Africa' signalled the approaching end of colonialism. John F. Kennedy's election as President of the United States spoke of new beginnings. Sean Lemass crossed the border to visit Terence O'Neill for the first meeting between an Irish Taoiseach and a Northern Ireland Prime Minister. There was flower power in the US and civil rights movements across the world. It was the era too of the angry young men who wanted

to change the world and to do so in a hurry. It was the era of dreams.

But somehow the dreams were never quite fulfilled. The civil rights movements in the North of Ireland threw up noble men like Hume and Mallon, but it also led to a revival of the IRA and the UVF with the awful consequences that followed.

And somehow it was gradually dawning on us that all was not well in the Republic either. There was a feeling that at least some of our politicians in positions of power were more interested in privilege than principle and were using their power to favour themselves and their friends. Was it late the 1970s or early 80s that George Colley warned of 'low standards in high places'?

Neither was all well within the Church. The high hopes engendered by the Vatican Council were not fulfilled. The ideals set out in the most inspiring documents of Vatican II, such as *Gaudium et Spes,* outlining the role of the Church in the modern world, or the document on ecumenism, suggesting the road towards unity between the Christian Churches, never became a reality.

I do believe that our Church during this period, and indeed all through the twentieth century, became too obsessed with what one might call personal holiness. There was a belief that to meet God and attain real holiness one needed to get away from society rather than taking an active role in it. There was little real connection between religion and daily life. This led to a privatisation of religion and placed morality very much in the private individualistic sphere.

There was, too, during that post 1960s period, a gradual lessening of confidence in the authority of the Church. In particular, aspects of its teaching on marriage, sexuality and family planning were being called into question, even by those who wanted to live their lives in accordance with that teaching.

The Celtic Tiger and Church Abuse Revelations

And then of course came the Celtic Tiger, and who could argue against it? Who could argue against jobs at home as opposed to the emigrant boat or plane? A recent report from the United Nations Development Programme ranked Ireland as the fourth richest country in the world with a per capita GNP surpassed only by the USA, Luxembourg and Norway. Economic growth, almost full employment, budget surpluses, new cars, foreign holidays, expensive shops and restaurants tell the story. It would be less than generous not to give credit to those who were principally responsible – the trade union movement, the employers and the government.

There is however another picture. Side by side with the new and prosperous Ireland there is a widening gap between rich and poor; run down inner-city estates, increasing homelessness among the young, and a frightening increase in the abuse of alcohol with all the accompanying consequences. There is growing aggression and violence on our streets, long waiting lists for medical care and public housing, and there is a two tier education system which has been highlighted in recent times. These are some of the visible, measurable flaws in the Celtic Tiger.

Further flaws, perhaps less measurable, have been emerging, adding to the erosion of confidence in our politicians. The downturn in the Celtic Tiger, and perhaps even more, the feeling that the news of its illness was kept from us as we approached the 2002 election, has given rise to increased distrust.

Recent tribunal findings have shown clearly that so many of the powerful people in our state, powerful politically and financially, have cynically used their power and privilege for their own personal gain. Flood and Moriarty, Ansbacher and, yes, our own banking institutions, the construction industry and brown paper bags all remind us that greed has caught hold of us.

Loss of trust in our politicians and in the political system, which somehow allowed or turned a blind eye to these abuses, is indeed significant.

Loss of trust, however, in the Roman Catholic Church, and especially in us bishops as leaders of that Church, has been much more dramatic. The scandal that a bishop could have fathered a child and concealed that fact for a further eighteen years of his Episcopal ministry was a major shock in the early 1990s. It is now regarded as something of a minor imperfection when compared with the more recent revelations of priests sexually abusing children and our apparent greater concern as bishops with protecting the 'good name' of the Church rather than the protection of children. These revelations have left many sincere Church people scandalised, angered and disillusioned. They have given further evidence to those already disaffected that the Irish Church is in the throes of death and good riddance to it.

Perhaps not all of the loss of trust is due to these more recent revelations. I do believe that some of the present hostility is also due to many hurts caused in the past by priests and bishops, but that the paedophilia issue has given a freedom to people to vocalise their hurt, in a manner which was not possible in the past. I have recently tried to bring healing to a family that was deeply hurt by Church authorities in a property dispute which occurred more than seventy years ago. The hurt had been transferred from parents to children, but only came to my notice following a Pilgrimage of Reconciliation across the diocese in preparation for the new millennium.

Loss of trust in those who would normally be expected to give leadership in values, who are expected to behave as if principle was always more important than privilege, has had serious consequences.

Story of a Soul: Where We are Now?

Loss of a Shared Vision and Language

I believe that it would be true to say that, through most of the century just passed, the great majority of Irish people operated out of an agreed vision – an agreed way of looking at life. There was a shared vision of faith and purpose in life, a knowledge of our past history and future hope. In recent years these old certainties of faith and culture have been eroded. There is a sense of rootlessness, of *carpe diem*, or if you can't *carpe diem* you at least do something exciting for the weekend if it is only to indulge in the oblivion of an alcoholic haze.

Even the old language, the very words, have taken on new meanings. Words like marriage, family, vision, mission, and the broad Church, so often mean what the user wants them to mean – like the Red Queen in Alice in Wonderland.

Loss of a Sense of Moral Responsibility

People of my age were reared with a strong sense of sin. In retrospect, that sense of sin was often oppressive and burdensome. God was a threatening figure from whom you could not hide and who was to be feared. The emphasis was very much on sexual mores – particularly from adolescence onwards – and the responsibilities to community had only a minor place. The moral life generally was a routine obedience to authority figures in the persons of local clergy and, I suppose, bishops.

I certainly have no yen to return to the old certainties. We appear, however, to have moved so far in the opposite direction that we are in real danger of losing any real sense of right or wrong. There is growing evidence of the privatisation of morality with the common adage 'his/her private life is his/her own affair'. There is little debate or discussion on morality, either private or public, or even if the distinction between public and private in the area of morality is valid at all.

The chief concern seems to be constantly on the state of the public finances, the GNP, unit cost, and efficiency – this is the new morality, these are the new gods. So much of the 2002 Nice Referendum debate focused on economics. So little focused on the Christian ideals of solidarity, of reaching out to the less well-off countries of Eastern Europe.

In this world of commerce there is an aggressive individualism in which the winner takes all and the loser goes to the wall.

Loss of Social Capital – Being Disconnected

Those of you who work with voluntary organisations will be aware that, in recent years, it has become increasingly difficult to find people willing to give of their time to these activities. Among the many reasons for this are longer working hours, longer commuting time, both partners working outside the home, and more time spent before the television screen. There is the added factor, particularly in the urban sprawl and in newer housing estates adjoining our towns, of what one might call disconnectedness.

Social capital is becoming a favourite phrase among the sociologists. A recent report from the Cork County Development Board attempted to describe social capital in a list of questions: Do you trust people? How many clubs, societies, social groups are you a member of? If your child gets sick do you have support to call on? Basically how much social contact do you have in your life? It tells us that these social ties, according to research, will help you to live longer and are worth money to the economy.

This growing phenomenon of disconnectedness is perhaps more obvious among the young. At a recent family gathering the Flood Tribunal Interim Report was being discussed – it had just been published. I noted that a bright twenty-year-old girl seemed to have opted out of the conversation. I asked her if she knew who Ray Burke was – she had no idea. She pointed out without any hesitation that she never reads newspapers and she does not listen to the news on radio or television. I have no doubt that if it was a matter of Church interest she would have been equally disconnected.

The disconnectedness of our young people is evident in the age profile of Sunday worshippers, and it is evident in the sizeable number of our young people who don't vote in elections. Is that disconnectedness related to the increased number of young people who have sadly taken their own lives in recent years?

Lack of Interiority – Of a Deeper Meaning to Life

A parish priest in North Tipperary died last year. His funeral was quite extraordinary; one sensed that this man was different. I sat down with a group of parishioners soon afterwards and asked them what was it about this priest that made him different. They spoke of his spirituality, of his reminding them of Christ. One man tried to sum it up: 'He saw a deeper meaning in things that we wouldn't see'. Interiority is, I believe, the word, that capacity to see the deeper meaning to the ordinary things in life, that sense of wonder, of reverence towards the mystery of life itself and the mystery of the events of each day. Some would call it a sense of God, others may speak of a sense of the great mystery which is life.

Story of a Soul: Where Might We Go from Here?

It is always easier to diagnose what is wrong than to prescribe what will put it right. I don't claim to have the solution to the ills that I have just pointed out. I do believe however that we very definitely need much debate and discussion in public and private in order to clarify our vision, our values, and our principles in a changing world.

We have spoken of the breakdown in trust and confidence in the two institutions that should be giving a lead in these matters – the Church and the State. Is there still a place of leadership in values for Church and State in our society? I believe there is but it is going to take time to rebuild the trust that has been broken. Someone said to me recently that it can take years to build trust, but it can be destroyed in a day.

I do believe that both Church and State must look at themselves very seriously and be prepared to take whatever radical action for change is necessary. I would be reluctant to tell the politicians how they too need to work towards restoring confidence in their leadership. I happen to believe that the vast majority of politicians are decent honourable people. Like us, they too are perhaps caught in a system or structure which needs re-examination. I happily leave it to them to ask the appropriate questions.

In regard to the Church, I believe we have to look at ourselves in a radically different way than we have been doing. I believe one of the greatest difficulties that the Church has made for itself is that it has seen itself in some way as an end in itself. The Church always came first.

Protection of the Church was more important than the protection of children. If anyone challenged Church authority, they were clearly wrong and had to be defeated – the Church could not be wrong. The leadership provided by the Church was leadership of authority, it was a privileged leadership.

Ultimately the Church must be at the service of the Gospel. The Gospel, the teaching and example of Jesus Christ, is the important thing. The Church has meaning and credibility only in so far as it is at the service of the Gospel. And if Christ came 'not to be served but to serve' then surely the Church and particularly those in leadership in the Church must be motivated by service. Its leadership must be servant leadership rather than privileged or authority leadership.

Part of that servant leadership rather than authority leadership must be the recognition that we do not have all the answers. We must be prepared to listen and take advice on the many positions which we thought were sacred. There are questions arising from the issue of sexual abuse which I don't like asking – the answers may be uncomfortable, but they must be asked.

- Has celibacy been a contributing factor in the area of abuse?
- Has our training as priests and religious in some way stunted our growth as sexual beings?
- Does priesthood attract more than its share of people with psychosexual difficulties?
- Have we as bishops in some way been more concerned about power and control than about service – above all service to the message of Christ?
- Have we as Church been too concerned with laws and orthodoxy and too little concerned with human development and human relationships?
- Have we neglected the supreme law – the law of love?
- Has the virtual absence of any female input into either Sacramental Ministry or decision making areas of Church been a serious distorting influence?

We need to seriously examine how we have trained and cared for those who are, as it were, the foot soldiers or perhaps foot servants of the local Church. The priests in the front line have suffered greatly in recent times. Many feel that they are paying the price for the abuses of privilege by others in the past.

Further questions need to be asked in regard to the wider issue of care of children. I do not wish in any way to minimise the awfulness of clerical sexual abuse when I note that the SAVI Report, Sexual Abuse and Violence in Ireland, April 2002, states that one in five females and one in six males experience sexual abuse in childhood. The authors of the report suggest that there is a pressing need for a comprehensive public awareness campaign combined with greater access to information for victims and professionals with the intention of removing the barriers to disclosure. As a society we need to respond much more proactively to these facts.

It is not good enough that this year between eighty and ninety child sexual abusers will be released from prison and less than ten of these have had the standard course of treatment while detained. Simple naming and shaming of abusers, venting of anger and acting out of revenge may be understandable, but contributes little to the reform of abusers or to the protection of children.

Story of a Soul – A New Beginning

If Church or State wish to regain the trust of people and to contribute significantly to the Ireland of the twenty-first century there is only one place for us to begin and that is with truth. We ought never to be afraid of truth.

Christ reminded us that 'the truth will set you free'. A society which does not value truth is a society where there cannot be trust. We have grown accustomed over the years to spin doctors and PR people who often appear more concerned with image rather than reality, with perception rather than truth. Yes of course there is nothing wrong with using people with expertise to help to explain, and to clarify, but when perception and image become more important than truth and reality, then we are in real difficulty.

Truth can be an elusive creature. I imagine that very few of us tell blatant lies, but what of the evasions, exaggerations, self-justifications, the withholding of information and the variety of other deceptions? Is there one of us who has never indulged in any of these?

Truth can be elusive. It can also be expensive. We have had a plethora of tribunals in recent times trying to find the truth about a variety of things. This has been at huge financial cost to the taxpayer. Is there something of an untruth about this very expensive search for truth?

The media of course occupy a very powerful role in the pursuit of truth. They have helped a great deal in pursuing the truth in political and Church spheres. The work of the media in uncovering the scandals of sexual abuse has been a significant service, albeit, a very painful one for us. But dare I risk saying the following to some of the media people? You have often and with real justification accused us in the Church of having used our power in an oppressive and uncompassionate manner in Irish society in the past. Can I ask you to be aware of the danger that you might use your power to occupy that oppressive and uncompassionate role which hopefully the Church has vacated or at least has begun to vacate?

Conor Brady, the recently retired editor of *The Irish Times*, put the challenge well in his parting address to his fellow journalists: 'Never forget the power we wield through that journalism. As journalists we have an immense capacity for doing good. We also have an immense capacity to damage, to injure, to hurt if we use our power carelessly, without regard to basic fairness, or in ways that are partisan or biased.' To work in the service of truth is indeed a privilege and a responsibility. If we work in the service of truth it seems to me that other values will automatically follow.

Sometimes truth can be painful when it challenges us to respond. One of the most painful truths in our world is the truth that we live in a society and in a wider world which is hugely unjust. It seems to me that the single greatest and most urgent challenge facing us in this new millennium is to begin to work seriously towards the creation of a just society and indeed towards a just world.

There has been much anger in recent times about our failure as bishops in responding to complaints of sexual abuse of children. That anger was justified and I believe ultimately constructive. We need similar anger about the threat of starvation of some eleven million people in the horn of Africa today.

Justice is not just about sharing the world's goods. Justice is above all else about right relationships. A just society is one which is structured in such a way as to promote right relationships between people, so that human rights are respected, human dignity is protected, human development is facilitated and the environment is respected and protected.

And of course justice is ultimately the only way to peace. One could speak of the values of solidarity, of courage, of compassion, and could I make a special plea for forgiveness? Would I be right in thinking that we are in danger of becoming a harsh and unforgiving people? There is not one of us in life who gets it right all the time; there is not one of us who hasn't done wrong; there is not one of us who is not at times in need of forgiveness.

To conclude, I have focused a good deal on the loss of trust in our major institution of Church and State and the consequent damage in terms of values and attitudes of people. Do not, however, think that I want to return to what is sometimes called 'the good old days' when we took trust in these institutions for granted. Much of what is being revealed today has its roots in those same 'good old days' when there was little or no accountability on the part of either institution.

Dickens was right when he said of his era 'it was the best of times and the worst of times'. He is still right. There is much to be hopeful about in today's Ireland. But we need the courage to promote the environment where informed debate can take place about where we are going as a people and what values we want to shape our lives. Those of us in positions of leadership may have to vacate our seats at the table of privilege and stand at the altar of principle. We need to be for ever searching for a soul for Ireland.

SOCIAL TRUST AND COMMUNITY CONNECTION

Robert Putnam

My wife Rosemary and I were first in Ireland twenty years ago. We were on vacation with our kids and we came to the west of Ireland and to Dublin. Now, of course, Ireland has changed dramatically. Irish people know that as much as anyone. It is an extraordinary change for a country to have gone through. I know that Ireland is in the midst of a debate about the implications of that experience. What are the political and social implications? What are the moral implications of that kind of transition?

I am not an expert on Ireland. I am an observer, but I do want to talk about what is going on in Ireland. I have spent a lot of time in many countries around the world, talking with people about issues of community, democracy and social justice, and I almost never say what I am about to say, that debate in this country is really of world class level. There is a very high level of expertise and sophistication in Ireland in discussions about community and social change, social justice, and so on. I admire that and you should be proud of it. Ireland is a real centre of learning, so I come here not to preach at you, but to talk with you about what has been going on in my country.

I want to give you a picture of what has been happening in America in the second half of the twentieth century, and leave it entirely open for discussion whether any of it or all of it applies to Ireland.

Firstly I want to ask what has been happening to the state of connections among people in the United States, to our connection with family and friends, community and institutions? The answer is that, by many different measures, there has been a substantial decline in human connections in the United States over the course of the last three decades. So the next question I will ask is why is that? What could possibly explain that? And as you will see, this is not an easy question. There is no single answer.

The third question is: So what? Does it really matter? Is this just nostalgia for the 1950s life? I argue that it really does matter, at least in the United States. In other countries, too, there is a lot of evidence that the connections we have with our family, friends, neighbours and community actually, in measurable terms, matter to the quality of, and indeed the length of, our lives. That leads me to the fourth question: What can we do in the United States or in any society to make sure that it has a vibrant social fabric?

I want to begin, however, with just a brief word about the concept of social capital. The core idea behind social capital is very simple: social networks – connections with other people – have value. We network and, in some sense, we can find out about what is going on in other parts of the country, and maybe we can find out about a job we might be interested in. Indeed, most people in the United States, and in most advanced countries of the world, get their jobs more through whom they know than for what they know. I am not talking about nepotism or corruption. I am just saying that most people don't find out about a job through ads in the newspapers, but rather we normally *get* jobs through networking. Your connections – your networks with other people – matter for your lifetime income. There is an economist at the University of Chicago business school who can calculate the dollar value to you of your address book. For most Americans, the dollar value of their address book is of greater value than all the degrees they have. In that sense, social capital has cash value. It has lots of other values too to people who are in the networks, which I will come to later.

In addition, social networks can have value even to people who are not themselves in the network. There are plenty of examples of this kind of effective social network, and one I am conscious of now is that my wife, Rosemary, and I have lived for many years in the neighbourhood of Lexington, Massachusetts. Lexington has a whole lot of social capital. People are all the time having barbecues and picnics, sledging parties and so on. And criminologists have shown that the best predictor of low crime in a neighbourhood is how many neighbours know one another's first names, because if there is a lot of connections then people keep an eye on one another's houses and so on. My wife and I are able to be here right now, confident that at this very moment our house back in Lexington is being protected by social capital, even though, and this is now the moment for confession, I actually never go to any of the picnics, or barbecues or sledging parties! I am not proud of that fact, but I am able to benefit from the networks even though I am not in them.

That is what economists would say are externalities of social networks. But the more important thing is that a social network often has consequences, not just for the people in them, but for the bystanders. One of the reasons for that consequence, that unusual feature, is that it turns out that in an organisation or in a community where there is a dense network of social connections – where people are connected to one another – what tends to evolve is a norm of reciprocity, generalised reciprocity. I know that sounds like a highfaluting term, but it just means that I will do something for you now without expecting something immediately back from you, because down the road you will do something for me, and you will do something for him, and we will all see each other at church on Sunday.

I know that reciprocity is a somewhat abstract concept. It was best defined by a rather famous American baseball player named Yogi Berra, who is a catcher for the New York Yankees. He once said that if you don't go to somebody's funeral, they won't come to yours. That is a deep thought. The longer you think about that the deeper that thought becomes. Yogi captured in that phrase the essence of reciprocity. So reciprocity is closely associated with people in social networks and that is one of the reasons why social networks are very valuable things to have.

That is all I mean by social capital. Social capital does not merely refer to non-profit organisations. That is a common misunderstanding. I happen to work for a non-profit organisation – Harvard University – and I can therefore testify that non-profit organisations are not always kinder or gentler places to work or live.

There is no connection between non-profits and status or civil society and social capital. Social capital is, in short, networks and reciprocity and what goes along with that, i.e. trust and trustworthiness.

Suppose I asked you to tell me to think of some community you know well, your hometown, for example. If I ask you to tell me what is the trend in social capital in that community over the last thirty or forty years, how would you figure that out? It would be difficult. You might ask a grandparent, but people's memories are fallible and there is always a risk of nostalgia affecting our judgment.

What I do for a living is count things. So, I got the idea that I could take advantage of the fact that organisations keep membership records – not all social capital is organisational, but some of it is. Since they keep membership records, we can look back and see what were the trends of membership in various organisations over long periods of time. We can look at, for example, how many Americans belong or have belonged, year by year, to Parent Teacher Associations – when there is a baby boom there are more parents and therefore more members of the PTA. We want to know not just how many members there are, but what business people call the 'market share'. Of all the people who could belong to an organisation how many did? Of all the parents in America, year by year, how many belonged to the PTA? Of all the kids in America, year by year, how many belonged to the Scouts? Of all the Catholic men in America, year by year, how many belonged to the Knights of St Columbus – an American Catholic men's organisation? Of all the Jewish women in America, year by year, how many belonged to Hadassah? Of all of the middle-aged American men, year by year, how many belonged to the animal clubs, that is, one of the men's organisations? Animal club refers to the fact that all men's organisations in America are named after animals – the Lions Club the Moose Club, the Elks Club, the Eagles Club, and so on.

So we look year by year at the membership of all those organisations, add all this up and we got an image of trends in organisational members. What you find is that for most of the twentieth century, Americans, year by year, were becoming more joiners. Year by year more and more parents joined the PTA, more and more kids joined the Scouts, more and more men joined their animal clubs and so on. There is only one great exception – the Great Depression. This had a really bad effect on social capital in America, at least in the short run, between 1930 and 1935. Many organisations in America lost half of their membership in those five years. But then coming out of the Great Depression, and especially coming out of World War II, there occurred probably the greatest civic boom in American history. Almost every organisation in America doubled its market share in the twenty years between 1945 and 1965.

Then suddenly, silently, and mysteriously, all of those organisations started experiencing a levelling of shares, then a slump of market shares and then a plunge in membership, until by the end of the twentieth century we are down again into Depression levels in terms of organisational activity. And that includes all sorts of organisations in America. Not every organisation hit the peak at exactly the same moment. The earliest organisation to hit its peak was the American Medical Association. Practically all doctors belonged to the AMA, which peaked in 1957. The last organisation to hit the peak was a civic group in America called the Optimists. They hit their peak in 1980 and then they just plunged. Now they are back down to the same as the rest of us.

This is a summary of the trends and social capital in America over the course of the twentieth century in America, but one is entitled to have doubts about it. First of all, it includes only card-carrying membership – it doesn't say whether people showed up or not. Secondly it could be suggested that these are all old-fashioned organisations. Every organisation mentioned has been around for a hundred years. But maybe it is just the old-fashioned organisations that are declining. We could call them the 'funny hat organisations', but maybe they have been replaced by other sets of groups that have sprung up to replace them like New Age poetry groups or Alcoholics Anonymous or something. So maybe we have stopped going to some of the old groups and started going to other groups?

One might also say, 'Wait a minute, just two minutes ago you said that not all social capital in America was organisational.' Maybe we have stopped going to organisations that are kind of old-fashioned. Maybe we are just connecting in other ways. Maybe we have stopped going to the Elks Club but we are going to bars and going on more picnics together, or something else not captured by the organisational membership. I have known for some time that that was a possibility. My problem is: I couldn't for the life of me figure out where the national picnic registry was kept. I said to myself, how would you ever know whether we are going on more or fewer picnics than we used to or than our parents did? Then the most exciting thing that has ever happened to me in my professional life occurred – I discovered two massive new data archives. You are saying to yourselves that this guy is a little weird. He gets off on data. I would like to persuade you that these are interesting sources of evidence. The first of these comes from a set of polls discovered after I began doing this work. It was discovered that the local survey organisation, every month for the last thirty years or more, has been asking a large national sample of Americans about their civic activities. The type of questions asked would include: Have you, in the course of the last twelve months, been to any public meeting where people talked about local affairs, school affairs or community affairs? Have you in the course of the last twelve months been an officer or a committee member of any local organisations? Have you in the course of the last twelve months, signed a petition? Have you in the course of the last twelve months run for office?

Now not that many Americans run for office, but this is a very large survey archive. There are half a million people in this survey archive. So we get good estimates of even quite rare behaviour like running for office. I can summarise for you the result of this archive very simply. Every single community activity that is measured in this survey is down over the course of the last thirty years. In 1973, 22 per cent of Americans had been to a meeting in the previous twelve months. By the middle or late 1990s, that had dropped to about 12 per cent and it is continuing to drop. This is not people's memory of what people used to do. It is actually comparing what people said in the 1970s to what people said in response to the same question in the 1990s. In 1973, 17 per cent of Americans had been an officer or a committee member of any local organisations and by the end that had fallen to about 8 per cent.

All of the survey shows you the same story. Over the course of the last three decades of the twentieth century about half of all of the civic infrastructure of American communities simply evaporated. Half of all the meetings, half of all the little local organisations, and so on. All sorts of organisations, not just the old-fashioned ones, disappeared.

That is, however, not the most interesting of the two survey archives that was discovered. We also discovered that a commercial marketing firm in Chicago, every year since 1975, has been gathering marketing data. They are an advertising firm, so gathering data on people's consumer preferences – do you prefer Ford company cars to GM cars or whatever – is important. But somebody in their advertising research office in 1975 came up with the idea that it would be useful to know, along with the consumer preferences, something about their lifestyle, because if you are trying to write an advertisement for a Ford motor, you would like to know if people who buy Ford motors ski a lot, or do they jog or whatever. So the surveyors started asking people questions about their lifestyle, not just about their consumer preferences. And they asked a series of questions, all of which have the same general format.

One of their clients was the Hallmark Greeting Card Company and they had the suspicion, which happens to be true, that people who go to church more often send more greeting cards. So they asked: How many times last year did you go to church? They also asked questions such as: How many times last year did you go to a club meeting? How many times last year did you go to a dinner party? How many times last year did you have friends over at the house? How many times last year did you go on a picnic? I had found the national picnic archive! And I can report to you as a verifiable fact that in 1975 the average American went on five picnics. Last year, however, the average American went on two picnics. America is in the midst of a national picnic crisis!

So what this survey did, what these hundred of thousands of people interviewed did, was to give us a veritable motion picture of recent changes in the American lifestyle. And I can summarize the relevant results very simply: Virtually every single form of social connection measured in this survey is down a lot.

In 1975 the average American went to twelve club meetings a year. By the late 1990s that figure had fallen to five club meetings a year. Most Americans don't go to club meetings at all. The decline in going to club meetings is greater than the decline in claimed club membership. Lots of people in America are carrying around cards saying that they are a member of such and such a club, but they never show up. Woody Allen had the right metric: 'Showing up is eighty per cent of life.'

In the United States as in Ireland, religion is a big part of social capital. Half of all American social capital is religious. Half of all membership organisations are religious. Interestingly, just about the same time we stopped going to club meetings we all began to stop going to church quite so often.

There is a long steady decline in attendance at church. Indeed, there is some evidence that the decline in church attendance in America is slightly understated. Sociologists have recently taken a rather interesting kind of research, asking people the same standard question: Did you go to church last week? And then they checked to see if you were actually in the pews. There are two interesting findings from this research. Firstly, lots of people misremember whether it was really last week that they were in church. Twice as many people say they were in the church as were in the pews. And secondly, there is some evidence that we are misremembering more than our parents did in response to the same question. So if you do go to church now, there are more phantoms sitting beside you in the pews, that is, people who think they are there but really aren't. Therefore, if we took out all the phantoms the decline in church attendance would be even greater. I have seen the equivalent figures for Ireland and the level of church attendance continues to be higher in Ireland than it is in the United States. It was much higher, but the decline in church attendance appears to be even greater in Ireland than in the United States.

So far I have been talking more about formal organisations like going to church, going to meetings, belonging to clubs and so on. But how about informal connections? I did mention picnics. There has been a decline of about 60 per cent in the frequency of dinner parties in America over this period. That is kind of consoling to my wife Rosemary and me because we have not actually been invited to a dinner party for the last decade and it was comforting to discover that nobody else is going to dinner parties either. But dinner parties already sounds kind of fifties. But how about having people just come over to the house? Does that sound fifties? In 1975 the average American had people come visit them in their home fourteen times and by the end of the century that had fallen to about eight times. All sorts of connections, for example playing cards, are largely a social activity. (A few people play solitaire, but it is not a big game.) In 1957 40 per cent of all American adults played bridge regularly. Last year that figure was 6 per cent and they are all in retirement communities. If you say bridge to an undergraduate audience in America today, it sounds to them the way whist does to us, in that it is a game you heard of, but you cannot imagine any breathing person playing it. Going by exactly the same data, if card playing of all sorts, not just bridge, continues the same steady trend that it has done for the past thirty years, the last card will be played in America in 2013 and you all will be able to see it – it will be televised around the world when the last card is played!

It is not just voting that is down. If I show you the figures for the present electoral turnout in America, which is right in line with the long and steady decline, you would think that maybe it is something political. That is why I am using examples like going on a picnic and playing cards. It is all of the various kinds of informal connections, including connecting with our own families, that are way down.

One of the questions asked in this survey is: How often do

you have dinner with your own family? There has been a decline of roughly 40 per cent in the frequency with which Americans have dinner with their own family. Breaking bread as the sun is setting with the people that you live with is a really old custom. We are in the midst of quite a momentous change in the way American families fit together. There has also been a decline in the frequency with which parents take vacations with their kids – a decline of roughly the same figures, 40 per cent. There is even a decline of about 40 per cent in the frequency with which Americans watch TV with their kids. It is not that Americans are watching TV any less. We are watching TV more than we used to, but everyone has their own TV sets so we are all watching TV alone. I thought about calling my book 'Watching TV Alone', but I didn't think it had quite the same pizzazz as 'Bowling Alone'.

There are many other ways in which this general phenomenon has made itself manifest. One is that we have become a less generous society. Americans, compared to other countries in the world, have historically been quite generous, in that we have given away a larger fraction of our income annually to good causes. The same period when we were joining up a storm, we were also being more and more generous, until in the same year that we stopped going to church and club meetings, we also stopped being quite so generous. Since then, there has been a more or less steady decline in our giving.

Another result of the survey– and I suppose that this is the core measure – is that we trust one another less. Would you say that most people could be trusted? In the 1960s more than half, approaching two thirds, of Americans said that most people can be trusted. Now that is down to one third of Americans. Two thirds say that you cannot be too careful. This trend in growing distrust is concentrated among America's young people, not because of some kind of epidemic of adolescent paranoia, but because, like the canary in the mine, America's youth are telling us that they are growing up in a less trustworthy society. It is not their fault – it is our fault. And that is, in some respects, the most poignant illustration of the point I am trying to make, which is that America's social capital reservoirs, which used to be really high by comparison to most countries in the world, have been drained quite a bit over the last thirty years.

So let us review. The first question was: What has been happening to American social capital over the second half of the twentieth century? For most of the twentieth century Americans were becoming more and more connected. It is not something that has been going on ever since we got off the Mayflower or whatever ship brought us there. But somehow, basically from around the time that I started to vote, America started to go to hell in a hand-basket. The second question I want to ask is why? Why this? Why have Americans become more disconnected? Are there multiple causes or is there just a single culprit?

I want to make clear from the outset that I don't know the answer. There are lots of great suspects. Some of the suspects look very suspicious and are actually very innocent – I am going to exonerate one or two very quickly – while some of the suspects are guilty as sin and I am going to indict them here. Let me begin with a couple I thought were guilty but turned out to be innocent. One of them was mobility: moving around a lot.

It is true that moving around a lot is bad for social capital. People who move around a lot have shallower roots, just like plants that get re-potted have shallower roots and communities that have a higher rate of mobility have a lower rate of social mobility. One reason that big metropolitan areas like Los Angeles or New York and, I suppose Dublin, have less social capital is because people move more often and their roots don't go down so deep. But that has nothing to do with the decline in social capital because America has been becoming, for the last six decades, a steadily less mobile society. Americans move less now than our parents and grandparents did. So mobility is not part of the story, even though it looked like a plausible suspect, it cannot have caused it because it hasn't changed in the right direction.

Political scandal is an interesting and challenging idea. It is possible to believe that the decline in voting turn-out might be related to Vietnam and to Watergate and Monica Lewinsky. However, it is hard for me to imagine that people have stopped going on picnics because they are still mad at Dick Nixon, or that there is some political explanation for their behaviour.

Some of the other suspects named are, on the other hand, quite relevant. Suburbanisation, for example. This was not on my list of top ten suspects when I began this research ten years ago. It turns out that there is a very simple rule of thumb: every ten minutes more of additional commuting time cuts all forms of social connection by 10 per cent. So ten minutes more commuting time, at least in the United States, means 10 per cent less church-going time, 10 per cent fewer dinner parties, 10 per cent fewer dinners with your family, 10 per cent fewer meetings. Twenty minutes more commuting time means 20 per cent less of all those things.

Regarding women working outside the home, my daughter, Lara, is a professional woman and a mom. She is someone I am very close to and she tells me that I have to be really careful in the next three sentences so that I don't give you the impression that she is personally responsible for the collapse of American civilisation. But it is true for guys my age that our moms were great social capitalists. They were out all the time connecting and so on and our wives and our daughters are out doing other great things. And we guys haven't picked up the slack. So part of this is a story of the movement of women into the paid labour force. But it is a much smaller part of the story than most people think. You can tell this because the same trends are equally down among stay-at-home moms. Actually the decline in membership to Parent Teacher Organisations is much greater with stay-at-home moms.

Television turns out to be an important contributor to the decline in social connectivity. To be sure, public affairs television is good for your civic health, i.e. watching the news at night, but most Americans don't watch the news. Most Americans watch *Friends* rather than have friends. Commercial entertainment television is lethal for social connection. TV itself has been a causal factor. It is not the only factor and sometimes when I talk to press people they think that television is my only villain, which is not true. Television is an important part of the story but it is not the only part of the story. Neither are computers responsible for causing these declines. The trends were going down for thirty years. Bill Gates was in diapers when the trends were going down. So the computers did not do anything to cause it.

Social scientists go about trying to solve things like this in the same way that the epidemiologist tries to solve a problem about an epidemic. You look for hot spots in the population, places in the population that have really been hit hard by the trend, and places that have been immune to the trend. I looked, for example, on whether the issue was caused by affluence, if the trends were any different among well-off people as distinct from among people who were less well off. And in fact the trends are identical. The trends are down among rich folk and down among poor folk and down at all levels of the income hierarchy. They are down among PhDs and they are down among high school dropouts. They are down among blacks and down among whites, and down among women and down among men, and they are down about the same among all these categories.

There is only one exception to that. The trends are not down among older people. The American data shows quite clearly that the group of Americans who came of age before or during World War II – basically my parents' generation – were much more socially connected. That is what Tom Brokaw, an American journalist, calls the greatest generation. I call it the long civic generation, but whatever its name, the lives of that World War II generation were all joined more. They gave more time, they gave more money, and they gave more blood. They went to meetings more, they went to church more, they voted more, and just like the energiser bunny, they are now in their eighties and they are still voting up a storm. That generation was terrific about civic engagement.

The only problem is, that they did not pass those traits onto their kids, the boomers, and their grandchildren, what we call the X generation. The gap, in terms of civic involvement, between the grandparents and grandchildren is enormous. So much of the decline in civic life in America is simply generational arithmetic. Every year we lose another slice of the most civically engaged part of American life and we add another slice of people at the bottom of the age hierarchy who are wonderful people, my own kids, but they don't have their grandparents' habits of civic connectedness.

And what happens in a society where there are these big generational changes? It is like you are driving down a street by a big church, but inside there is dry rot. For a long time you don't notice it until one day it just collapses. And that is what is happening to much of civic life in America, and now it is happening to our civil organisations. It means you cannot just tell from the outside. You need to know what is going on in the dynamics of membership.

Let me now put forward the third question. Does it really matter if we are not connected? We can get along without social connections, you might argue. We don't need to have grandma around to raise the kids because we can pay for day-care. We don't need connections in order to find our mates because we can go to a dating service, or we can use financial capital to make up for the social capital we are missing. I believe that view is very wrong – and not for sentimental reasons.

In many measurable ways our societies don't work as well where we are not connected with one another. I have already given one example of that earlier when I talked about the connection between the crime rate and connectedness. There are other examples. Schools, for example, demonstrably don't work as well where parents are not involved in the educational process. If you had to choose between two strategies for improving schools you could either spend 10 per cent more on schools, smaller classes, more computers and so on, or have 10 per cent more parental involvement in the schools. No question, the latter is the better strategy for effectively improving scores in schools.

I am not saying that we shouldn't spend more money on schools; don't misunderstand me. My wife is a public school teacher so I have a vested interest financially in paying teachers well! I am saying that the reason why American test scores have fallen as they have over the last thirty years is not schools – it is parents. We have a parents problem not a schools problem in the United States.

I want to close this third part by saying that there are powerful physical health effects of social isolation. Your chances of dying over the next twelve months are cut in half by joining one group. They are cut by three-quarters by joining two groups. As a risk factor for death and ill health, social isolation – and I don't mean living in a cave someplace, I mean not knowing your neighbour – is as big a risk factor for death as smoking. If you smoke and belong to no groups it is a close call as to which is the most dangerous behaviour. And if you do smoke, by all means you should join a couple of groups to make up for that.

I don't want to be practising medicine without a license here, but to be serious, what I am saying is that this is an area where there is active research. I have just been to a couple of conferences in the last couple of weeks of serious medical folks, looking at why it is that social connections seems to have a very powerfully positive effect on health. Part of it is apparently what we call 'social support', that if you go to the church every week and then someday you slip and fall in the bathtub someone is more likely to notice if you are not at church. But part of it is not only that. Part of it is apparently physiological changes; there are blood chemical changes if you are connected with other people, so that if you are around other people, what is called 'stress buffers' build up in your blood. This is probably the sentence in the whole talk that you will find the most hard to believe: going to meetings is good for your stress level. So next time you call a meeting and somebody complains you can say, 'I am doing this for you. It is going to be good for your life expectancy!'

To be serious again, there is a connection between the trends in youth suicide in the United States and these trends. Social isolation is a big predictor of depression. This is not only in the United States. The United States and other countries are in the midst of a depression epidemic. I don't mean just feeling a little blue or going to the shrink. Clinically measured depression has increased tenfold in America over the last thirty years and is directly linked to social isolation which is directly linked to the suicide epidemic among young people. Among the civic generation there has been a fall in suicide because they are connected.

So what I have been trying to say here is that being connected really matters. When we talk about social capital we are sometimes accused of nostalgia for the past and that is not true. We are talking about real measurable changes, benefits that flow from connecting with other people. So what do we do about this?

I have described this great plague that has come right across the United States. I don't know how to fix it, but I do have a way of thinking about it and possibly this is also relevant to Ireland. In a nutshell, over the course of the last generation or two, a variety of technological, social and economic changes have rendered obsolete a stock of American social capital. Now go back a hundred years in American history. Go into the time machine with me. We go back and it is the early 1900s. We get out of our time machine and we are in Boston. The first question we would ask in that situation is how social capital is doing. And what you would find is that the same thing was true then.

America at the turn of the last century had just been through thirty or forty years of dramatic technological and economic changes that rendered obsolete their stock of social capital. In that case it was urbanisation, industrialisation and immigration, which meant that when people moved from the village to the city, whether the village was in Iowa or in County Clare, they left behind much of their family and their community institutions. All over America, people faced a social capital deficit. They didn't use this language of course, but there was a lack of community. They described it as a spiritual disconnection.

America in 1900 was a whole lot wealthier than it had been in 1870. They had just been through the industrial revolution after all and people were living materially much better than their parents could ever dream of. They had nifty gadgets that their parents could never have imagined. The telephone was actually a niftier gadget for them than the Internet is for us. They were much better off materially, but they felt disconnected and they felt isolated. There were whole passages of literature written around that time that could be republished now and you would think they were written about our times in America – the sense of disconnection in the midst of plenty.

Then they fixed the problem. In a very short period of time, at the turn of the last century, most of the major civic institutions that are in American life today were invented. In about ten or fifteen or twenty years the Boy Scouts, the Red Cross, the League of Women Voters, the National Association for the Advancement of Coloured People (the major African American organisation in America), the Rotary Club, the Lions Club and most Labour Unions were founded. It is hard to name a major civic institution in American communities that was not invented within about twenty years. If you had been around then it would have been tempting to say life was much nicer back on the farms where everybody knew everybody. But that is not what they did. A group of determined, creative, energetic, optimistic social reformers created, across America, a whole new set of ways of connecting.

Similarly, if you heard the first part of my remarks about the down trends, you might be tempted to say, to my horror, and embarrassment, that I was saying that life was much better back in the fifties. Will all women please report to the kitchen! And turn off the TV on the way. That is not what I am saying. I do not want to return to the fifties. Instead I think we, in America, need to reinvent new ways of connecting that fit in to the way that we have come to live and this will involve changes at the grass roots. It will also involve initiatives by government. One of the reasons I hang out with people in government is that I am trying to get them to make policy changes in America. Changes, for example, that will affect the balance between work and life, i.e. how do we fit work and life obligations when both parents are working outside the home. That is partly a problem for employers and it is partly a problem for government. Also there are things that people can do. There are things that need to be done at the grassroots in reweaving the fabric of our society. Most of the ideas from the last time that we solved this problem a hundred years ago did not come from Washington, and they certainly did not come from Harvard. They came from ordinary people in ordinary cities all across America trying to find out new ways to connect with people they did not know so well, but thought they should know better.

Finally, in the debate about social capital in the United States and perhaps elsewhere, sometimes people pose the social capital issue as if one has to make a choice between a social justice agenda and a social capital agenda. Either we can worry about inequality, some people say, or we can worry about bowling leagues. That is the wrong way of tackling the problem because there is a very strong positive correlation between social capital and equality. Across the American States, from State to State, the places that have the smallest gap between the rich and poor are the same places that have the highest level of social capital. Across the countries of the world, the places in the world that have the highest level of social capital, Sweden and Norway, have the lowest gap between rich and poor. The places that have the biggest gap between rich and poor – Brazil for example – have the lowest level of social trust. In periods in America where we have had a sense of social capital and connection, we have had also a small gap between rich and poor. Why is that? Well it could be that the inequality enables us to connect. I am sure that is part of it. But also part of it is that in a society where we have connections with other people, we have a more capacious sense of 'we' so that pursuing those policies that pursue social justice doesn't seem so much like pure altruism. We are all in this together.

But what is wrong most of all about this decline in social capital in America is that we don't see ourselves as all being in the same boat anymore. The only way, I believe, that we are going to have sustained political support in the United States, and perhaps in other countries, for aggressive policies to reduce inequalities and increase social justice is if we reweave the fabric of our communities and begin to see ourselves in other people, who otherwise don't look as if they belong to us. We need a more capacious sense of "we."

So the challenge I think for my country, and maybe other countries, is figuring out new ways to create this wider sense of us, new ways of connecting with other people, formally and informally, and reweaving the fabrics of our societies. Not in the old traditional way, maybe using some of the old traditional values, but not in the old traditional ways, but in new ways that will last us and our kids for decades.

AN
INTER-GENERATIONAL
CHALLENGE

A FRAMEWORK FOR
A NEW REALITY: 1

John Abbott

What, you may well be wondering, could have conspired to bring a father and son team to stand up in front of you at the conclusion of this most important conference on values and ethics? The simple answer is that, some four years ago, I was struggling to complete the writing of an autobiographical description of my search to better understand how it is that humans learn. My usual verbosity meant that I was actually struggling to reduce the manuscript by 40 per cent and in an inspired moment I turned to Peter, who was about to go to Cambridge to read English, for help in précising.

As he worked on this, and as I finally decided to use Wordsworth's evocative phrase 'the child is father of the man' as its title, it seemed appropriate to suggest that Peter should write a postscript. He drove a hard bargain – he would only do it if I agreed in advance not to edit anything he wrote. With some slight qualms I agreed.

I should not have worried – it has been his postscript that has been reprinted in journals far more frequently than anything I wrote! Then Harry Bohan read it. He was fascinated. And so here we are, both of us just a little nervous. We have not done such a double act before.

I have always believed that if something important is not

working out as it should, then it's my personal responsibility to stand up and do something. Not that this gives me a messianic status, but the sum of many 'insignificant' people acting together can move empires, as Gandhi so obviously demonstrated.

There are two things I wish to talk about: value systems, and the process of learning. I hope to show you that they are both about a major moral issue – our respect, or lack of respect, for young people.

Early in life I learnt from my father that I had to play my part in making a difference. My father had intended to be an engineer until, in his last year at school, he decided to be ordained. To me he was as impressive in his workshop down in the vicarage cellar constructing all kinds of wonderful Heath Robinson-like contrivances, as he was delivering simple but powerful sermons. Himself the son of a yeoman farmer from Devon he embodied to me, as his son, all that rich oral and practical tradition of the craftsman developing an apprentice – determined that his apprentice son would one day be more skilled than himself.

I doubt if he ever knew – for he died young – of the American Indian proverb: *We have not inherited this world from our parents; we have been loaned it by our children.* But he would immediately have concurred, because he always taught me that the older generation was answerable to the next generation. I think modern society is in danger of having completely forgotten that; we tend to blame young people for what is, in practice, our own inability to properly inculcate them with what it means to be a responsible adult.

My father was, in some ways, a tough taskmaster. He would rarely answer my questions directly, preferring to turn them back on me by saying, 'Well, how would YOU explain that?' My job, he believed, was to work things out for myself; when I fell he would, of course, pick me up.

Yet it was a ten-year-old boy who, when I was twice his age, gave me my most significant spiritual insight.

It happened like this. I was filling in time before going to university (TCD) by teaching in a small boarding prep school. Inexperienced as I was, I had to feed on my enthusiasms to keep the lessons going, and that was hard. One Friday afternoon I just ran out of steam. 'Let's have a debate about space travel,' said the class of ten-year-olds. I agreed, anxiously watching the clock and willing the last bell to ring. There was a lively discussion.

Then one boy said out of the blue, 'What would people look like on another planet?' The class was silenced; save for one boy who got very excited and waved his hand so vigorously in the air that I had to let him answer.

'I know, I know,' he said. 'They would look just like us.'

The class groaned – what a stupid answer. Timothy, the youngster concerned, was desperately upset and was close to tears. Gently I moved to help him out. 'Tell us, Timothy, why you think they would look like us.'

He perked up. 'Well, Sir, it's easy. In the Old Testament it says God made man in his own image and so if we look like God, so must they.'

The rest of the class was silent, and then the bell rang. It was my turn to be perplexed. None of my father's sermons had put it as clearly as that.

Now I have never attempted – thankfully – to be as literal as that. I know no more about what God looks like than any of us here today, and I probably have as many difficulties as any of you in defining what form Deity might take. But to regard every human creature as 'being in the image of God' – to be an aspect of the Divine, however you define it – is to elevate our relationships with another to the realms of the sacred.

Society is, however, fast losing that reverence for the 'specialness' of every individual.

I spend much of my time studying the latest research from neurobiology, cognitive science and evolutionary studies, to synthesise just what it is that we know with a degree of certainty about human innate predispositions to act in particular ways. These findings, at one level, reflect exactly what Adam Smith knew, what so many Eastern religions tell us, and what Genesis tells us about the quarrel between Cain and Abel – we are a confused species capable of great acts of altruism, and the most terrible acts of cruelty. We are competitive as well as collaborative. Every moment of every day we have to make decisions, we have to discriminate between what we think is right and what, through natural law or perceived culture, we see as wrong.

Such decisions are impossible to make without some sort of framework, a set of good stories if you like, that set the pace for individual choice within a culture.

A score of years ago I had a thesis bubbling in my head that I never really followed up. It went something like this. *When the proportion of the population who believe that their reward will come in some form of the Hereafter falls below a certain level then the dominant 'mene' in that society becomes the search for rewards in the Here and Now.*

I don't know what that proportion is, but I suspect it was never very high (as a species we are not good at delayed gratification). But I'm certain we have fallen below that level. Above the line, as it were, the influence of altruistic believers suggests a code of behaviour for the majority in which greed is not acceptable; below that line and everybody sees it as being acceptable to go all out for number one. 'You only live once,' we say.

What has happened to the Seven Deadly Sins, those antisocial behaviours that the medieval world defined as being destructive of civilised behaviour? Have you noticed how capitalism now uses every one of them as drivers for material growth? What was once defined as bad is now defined as good: it may help the economy, but it wreaks havoc with our present lives.

It shouldn't have taken the evolutionary psychologist, Kenan Malik, in his book *Man, Beast or Zombie?*, to remind us that we are, as social beings, more than simply the 'beasts' that evolutionary studies might suggest – trapped as we are in our ancestral urges – nor are we simply intelligent machines as defined by cognitive science.

John Eccles, the Cambridge Nobel Prize winning neurobiologist cautioned us: 'The human mystery is incredibly demeaned by scientific reductionism … we are spiritual beings with souls in a spiritual world, as well as material beings with bodies and brains existing in a material world.' We are in danger of losing that humanitarian vision, says Malik: 'Which is as much a consequence of our culture's loss of nerve, as it is to scientific advance'.

So how are we educating the next generation to make good decisions, to steer our Stone Age instincts through the intricacies of the early twenty-first century? This is where I come to my second issue – the process of education.

'Thinking things through for yourself' is a deeply engrained human instinct, which generations of craftsmen, like my father, have struggled to encourage over the generations. Inquisitiveness is one of the three or four key instincts that we have inherited from our ancestors that make possible our survival from generation to generation. The more you can think things through for yourself the more in control of your future you become.

Evolutionary studies show us that for several millions of years our minds and bodies evolved within small groups. For most of our ancestors, until the late eighteenth century, successful living meant knowing how to exist alongside a group of little more than fifty people – the farm, the shop, the ship, the craft workshop, or whatever. Within this, everyone had to learn how to turn their hands to most things – they had to successfully multi-task, as told most compellingly in the story of Swiss Family Robinson.

Towards the end of the nineteenth century, when in America 'big' was seen as 'beautiful', industrial growth was inhibited, said the young engineer Frederick Winslow Taylor, by the idiosyncratic practices of craftsmen. Thinking things out for yourself was, Taylor argued, 'unscientific'. Effective production, Taylor believed, meant treating men as if they were machines because 'technical calculation' (in Taylor's terms this meant doing things by the rule book) is in all respects superior to human judgment.

Scientific management vastly improved profits, and increased wages, but alienated workers: 'You leave your brain at the door when you work at Ford,' said a bitter craftsman. But the human spirit is indomitable: 'Trouble is,' mused Henry Ford himself, 'when I hire a pair of hands I get a thinking human being.' Fritz Schumacher commented, 'soul-destroying, meaningless, mechanical, monotonous, moronic work is an insult to human nature ... and no amount of bread and circuses can compensate for the damage done.'

Yet for a hundred years society has been seduced by 'economies of scale' and in scientific management – telling people what to do rather than letting them work it out for themselves – society has vastly increased its material rewards at the cost of 'dumbing people down'.

Education systems – whether in the US, Ireland, Australia, South Africa or in England – rapidly adopted such scientific management techniques from as early as the 1920s, first as an economic way of providing education for the masses and more recently (as seen presently in England since the Educational Reform Act of 1988) as a way of rapidly raising achievement scores. In country after country school courses are being extended, content levels increased, and instruction has come to dominate thinking it out for yourself.

'It's the only way we can get through all the material,' plead hard-pressed administrators. Oscar Wilde would have had a field day. Do you remember his definition of a cynic? 'The person who knows the price of everything and the value of nothing.'

Youngsters dislike all this intensely. To them it just doesn't seem the right way to learn. For a dozen or more years there have been bio-medical technologies able to scan the functioning of the brain which are beginning to explain not only why this doesn't feel right to the adolescent but, even more significantly, what is the long-term damage being done to the youngsters – damage that is already wreaking havoc in society.

Very briefly let me explain. As a species we are born with relatively tiny brains (if this were not so the baby's head would never get down the birth canal). Our species' evolutionary achievement is that we are born with a vast array of innate predispositions to learn rapidly through interaction with our environment. Note, however, that these predispositions, shaped over millions of years as being techniques that help us grow our brain in ways that facilitate our survival, are innate. They don't develop unless stimulated by their environment. As we use our brain so we shape it.

You all know about the apparently miraculous learning capabilities of children below the age of five or six to learn by a process that can only be described as osmosis. In the world we come from, where for millions of years you were old at twenty and dead by twenty-five, this accelerated learning was essential for survival. But just to 'soak up' skills and knowledge from the environment doesn't give anyone the capability to think things out for themselves – to find imaginative ways around new problems. Nature has provided for that in the second of three periods of neurological restructuring that we call adolescence. Modern society, tragically, seems more frightened than excited by adolescents.

Biologically this is strange. The energy of adolescents, its sheer bloody-mindedness if you like, the experimentation with new ideas that we fear will lead to risky behaviour, is an essential part of the weaning of the individual's dependence on other people. It is also a key part of society's resources to deal with change. Adolescents come to adulthood through learning to balance intellectual correct reasoning (the skills learnt around the campfire or in a classroom) with practical risk-taking skills,

Such synaptogenesis in adolescence is, like inherited predispositions, probably time bound – roughly between the ages of 13 and 18. Like other predispositions however if you don't use it you lose it.

Here, I believe, the influence of Winslow Taylor's 'scientific management' when applied by educational administrators in a hurry is disastrous for the human race. That's an extraordinary claim.

What do I mean?

Because our societies too frequently confuse information acquisition with education we have started to so extend the years of schooling and so fill these years with formal instruction, that we have by-passed the individual adolescent's deep-seated desire to think it out for himself. If the adolescent is not allowed to do this when his or her innate predispositions are struggling to express themselves, we should not be surprised when, after three, four or five years of university, the young adult may have all the paper qualifications in the world but he or she can't organise a piss-up in a brewery!

That may sound flippant, but I am actually deadly serious. While the human race is without doubt the planet's pre-eminent learning species, we make the most awful mistakes if we see schooling and instruction as the dominant contributors to brain growth. They are not.

Lenin was one of Winslow Taylor's greatest advocates. He applied scientific management both to rebuilding the Soviet economy and to purging Russia of freethinking intellectuals, amongst whom were the religious leaders. To help oppressed congregations refute such 'dumbing down' Pope Pius XI in 1931 proclaimed the Doctrine of Subsidiarity, which says, 'It is wrong for a superior body to hold to itself the right to make decisions for which an inferior is already well qualified to make for itself'.

As someone passionately concerned that there is something in the underlying principles that Western countries are applying to education that seems to result in the most awful unintended consequences of narrow thinking, dependency and a sense of unreality from world problems, I believe the Doctrine of Subsidiarity shows just what this is. We have so 'overschooled' youngsters that they are not properly 'educated'.

As teachers (including the very best) or parents (including the very best), we are nothing like as good as we should be in letting our young charges do things for themselves. I find the Doctrine of Subsidiarity most helpful when articulating what should be the proper *evolving* relationship between teachers and pupils, and between parents and child.

That is what I, as a father first and foremost, feel is my prime responsibility for my children. It is also the model I have sought to apply to other people's children, entrusted to me within a classroom. For many years now I have come to realise that a very major problem in formal education – indeed I think it is at the root of all the other problems – is the over dominance of the teacher (and of the caring parent) over the child wanting to exercise such a right to do it for himself.

This is where each of us has to think very carefully about the Doctrine of Subsidiarity. It should be the end point of the intellectual weaning process. By 'end' I don't just mean the final act. I mean it should be the 'end' or the 'aim' of the whole education process. It is a moral injunction as well as an organising principle. Subsidiarity has to start when children are very young. Leave this sense of self-control too late and a sense of dependency (intellectual laziness) creeps in; this is not just I as the pedagogic speaking – this is the inevitable biological consequence of trivialising children.

It was not the late twentieth century that invented the concept of 'lifelong learning'. We have simply attempted to rescue, from the desolation of the industrial approach to intelligence over the past two hundred or so years, what is an intrinsic human predisposition – namely the ability, and the desire, to work things out for ourselves. In this rescue process, however, we seem poised to make another mistake. Late twentieth-century educators have seen the opportunity to extend the institutional provision of education on a scale hitherto unthought of: university lecture halls for 50 per cent of the population of late teenagers! Our Stone Age ancestors would have gone crazy!

We are in danger of missing the point. A point we have actually understood for many years, but done little about. If children were to receive, when young, an education that consciously sought to give them a progression of skills and attitudes which, as they grew older, would put them more in charge of their own learning and make them less dependent on teachers for instruction, this would release that deep-seated urge 'to do it for myself'. To be responsible. It's what maturity is all about.

I would like to reverse the current assumption that we, in England and in many other countries, do have a problem with our children, especially teenagers.

I would suggest we rephrase this: teenagers have a problem with us because we just don't know when to let them take over. Why? Because, deep down, we know that we never gave them the skills when they were very young that would give them both the confidence and the competence to do so when they are older.

It's a problem of our own making because we have never really understood the tenet of subsidiarity.

We compound this because we have lost our moral bearings. We have to rediscover our humanity – we have to reposition ourselves and understand why it is we are more than just evolved animals or intelligent automata; we are conscious beings faced with the challenge of making sense of ourselves.

We have to look more carefully at ourselves, rather than simply blaming the teenagers, and accept that if youngsters are currently confused about their cultures and values, that's our fault, not theirs. In a sense it is *we*, the older generation, who still have to grow up.

A FRAMEWORK FOR A NEW REALITY: 2

Peter Abbott

'We must love one another or die.' The poem in which these words first appeared, 'September 1st, 1939' by W. H. Auden, was widely quoted in the days and weeks following the terrorist attacks of September 11th. It's easy to see why. 'I sit in one of the dives,' the opening lines of the poem read, 'On Fifty-second Street.'

> Uncertain and afraid
> As the clever hopes expire
> Of a low dishonest decade:
> Waves of anger and fear
> Circulate over the bright
> And darkened lands of the earth,
> Obsessing our private lives;
> The unmentionable odour of death
> Offends the September night.

Despite its oft-repeated citation, journalists and commentators, seeking to inject their stories with an example of their urbanity and well-read intellect, missed, I think, perhaps the most important theme of Auden's work.

A few lines later, he writes: 'There is no such thing as the State / And no one exists alone.' Here, I think, lies the centre of the poem, the central idea that Auden struggled with for much of his life, and the centre and meaning of what we have all gathered here to discuss. That is the relationship of ourselves, our own individualities, our own aloneness, to other men and women, to the societies or, in Auden's terms, to the states – be it families, universities, offices, or nations – in which we count ourselves members. For it is these relationships, these essential connections that bind us to each other, that inform and guide whatever it is that we call our values and ethics.

I started with Auden both because of his ultimate message, and because of the connection that was made between him and September 11th. Because, at its very root, that disaster that has shaped so much of our political and social discourse over the past year, is all about connections and relationships, and, of course, the lack thereof.

It was, as President Bush told us, an act of evil. In his first press conference after the attack, Bush mentioned 'the evil one' and 'evildoers' five times. He later vowed that 'across the world and across the years, we will fight the evil ones, and we will win.'

Such a simple demarcation flies directly in the face of all that we know. Alexander Solzhenitsyn writes in *The Gulag Archipelago*: 'If only there were evil people somewhere insidiously committing evil deeds and it were necessary only to separate them from the rest of us and destroy them. But the line dividing good and evil cuts through the heart of every human being.'

The radical critic and academic Raymond Williams asserts that 'evil, as it is now widely used, is a deeply complacent idea. When we abstract and generalise it, we remove ourselves from any continuing action and deliberately break both response and connection.'

It is that last word, 'connection', that I want to focus on.

In one definition, the only definition that I think is really valuable now, evil is seen as a lack of empathy for others, a basic inability to identify another's existence with your own. It is, in short, a lack of connection.

Writing shortly after the attacks on New York and Washington, the novelist Ian McEwan wrote: 'If the hijackers had been able to imagine themselves into the thoughts and feelings of the passengers, they would have been unable to proceed. Imagining what it is like to be someone other than yourself is at the core of our humanity. It is the essence of compassion and the beginning of morality.'

September 11th is important in other illustrative ways as well. It was at once a very modern affair and a very primeval one. The terrorists showed great media savvy, but the terror they inflicted was as old as Cain and Abel. Osama bin Laden is the very model of a modern businessman with a wide variety of interests worldwide, but continually preaches anti-Western, anti-capitalist rhetoric. There was video footage of Iraqi children celebrating the attacks, but they were wearing Michael Jordan t-shirts. The attacks were apparently the first salvos in a clash of civilizations, East versus West, but just how much Western culture has been influenced by the medical, literary and astrological advances of the East was, of course, at best not referred to and at worst not even understood.

September 11th was a text-book example of how close we have all become, and how far away from each other we still are.

In many ways we are now more closely connected than ever before. A couple of days ago I was sitting at my computer and a friend sent me an instant message. It popped up on my screen: 'Are you there?' it asked. I wrote back 'Yes', and immediately the response came back: 'Pick up the phone.' My phone rang, and it was my friend wanting to discuss the results of his latest date with a girl that he likes. Later that day, the phone rang again. It was another friend asking me which room number I was in. I told him, and immediately my doorbell rang. He had been standing outside and wasn't sure which button to press!

Okay, these are pretty piddling examples, but I think they're illustrative of a broader point. Our lives, at least the lives of those fortunate enough to be able to afford the luxuries of computers and mobile telephones, are saturated with potential for communication.

We know, for example, that our choice of coffee affects the lives of coffee growers in Honduras. We know that the clothes on our backs could well have been made from the labour of children living on less than a dollar a week. We know that the banks in which we place our money may be investing it in companies whose plundering of the earth's natural resources may, eventually, leave us biologically homeless. The Marxist critic Terry Eagleton writes that 'In the dense intermeshing of human affairs, it is no simple matter to decide whether an action is mine or not, or to unravel the unfathomably complex effects bred by a single act of one's own in the lives of others.' The web of connectivity between our normal, humdrum lives and the farthest reaches of the planet is clearer than ever before. Despite this, knowing about this connectivity does not necessarily equate to doing something about the deficiencies and inequalities we see because of that knowledge. How many people still drink coffee at Starbucks, wear clothes made by Gap, invest with Barclays? I know I still do all three, and I consider myself fairly well informed. Despite the efforts of many to bring these connections to our attention, the human heart finds it hard to empathise with those so far removed. We're aware that the connections exist, but they remain abstractions, almost impossible to fully grasp. They've become, like so much static, part of the incessant broadcast of modern life. Like a television left on in the other room, we hear the words and sounds but dimly, preferring to concentrate on other things instead.

This half-hearing can't continue for much longer.

In July, a study by the World Wildlife Fund gave Planet Earth, our home, a mere fifty years to live. Humankind's inexhaustible lust for consumption has doubled since 1970 and continues to accelerate by 1.5 per cent a year. The human population exceeded the Earth's sustainable capacity around 1978. Whilst it takes 12.2 hectares to support the average American and 6.28 for each European, it takes only 0.5 hectares to support each citizen of tiny Burundi. If the rest of the world – to put this in perspective – were suddenly to reach American levels of consumption, we would require four more planet Earths on which to live.

The scientist Fritjof Capra writes: 'Our complex industrial systems ... are the main driving force of global environmental destruction, and the main threat to the long-term survival of humanity.'

Because of corporate influence, it is the assets of companies, rather than the assets of nations, that are measured and discussed. What is not discussed by these giddy cheerleaders of capitalism is the fact that the two hundred richest corporations command resources equal to the combined wealth of the poorest 80 per cent of the world's population. Or the fact that the assets of the world's three richest people exceed the combined GNP of all least-developed countries and their six hundred million souls.

In one of Arthur Miller's earlier plays, *All My Sons*, he explores the connections between the private world of one family and the wider world of a nation. Joe Keller, the head of the family, works in a munitions plant and knowingly ships off defective parts to the air force. Tragedy occurs, and the moral of the drama is obvious: it embodies, in Miller's words, 'the concept of a man's becoming a function of production or distribution to the point where his personality becomes divorced from the actions it propels.'

We have seen and will, I fear, continue to see, the effects of this divorce.

The reasons for our perceived inability to connect with others are diffuse. It is partly a decline in community, as Robert

Putnam points out in *Bowling Alone*. A loss of ability to connect within our own immediate neighbourhoods is hardly going to help us connect on a wider level. It is partly an excess of information as I hinted at earlier. Too many sound-bite driven news stories on devastation in Bali, or the latest victim of the Washington sniper, immures us against too much emotional involvement in a particular issue and so we involve ourselves emotionally in none.

But it is also a failure of morality.

Not a failure of morality in the sense that some of the right-wing English tabloids, or Deep South bible-bashing Christians, would have you believe.

It is a basic failure of moral *imagination*.

Here I want to talk a little bit about the life-ordering and imagination-building powers of myth. It is a concept that our at all times rational world has pushed far, far away, pushing with it, I fear, the regenerative and inspirational powers of religious belief.

Friedrich Nietzsche wrote at the end of the nineteenth century that 'myth, the necessary prerequisite of every religion, is already paralysed everywhere.' He understood quite clearly how much religion depended on its mythological foundations, its roots in mystery and the unknown. He knew that when, and I quote, 'the mythical premises of a religion are systematised as a sum total of historical events ... the feeling for myth perishes, and its place is taken by the claim of religion to historical foundations.'

Although the religious establishment has soaked history in blood for too long, the narrative and explanatory power of religious myth has brought great happiness and succour to millions. Religious mythology is profoundly effective in helping men and women impose order on otherwise random events. It helps, in short, to rescue them from chaos and confusion.

Religious myth, however, no longer serves to exercise our moral imagination. Modern Christian thought must bear its own responsibility for smothering the mythical and narrative power of Christianity with orthodoxy and dogma (the recent arguments surrounding the new Archbishop of Canterbury or the Chief Rabbi, Jonathan Sacks, are emblematic of a worrying new trend). Modern Christianity has, quite simply, failed its adherents.

Perhaps there's a radical way out of the impasse. 'The attempt by humans to discover a morality apart from God,' writes Richard Holloway, former Bishop of Edinburgh, 'might, paradoxically, be God's greatest triumph; and our attempt to live morally as though there were no God might be the final test of faith.'

It is clear to me, I think, that there needs to be at the very least a re-thinking of the concepts of morality and ethics that we have grown up with. With the world so apparently 'out of joint', with our moral imaginations being taxed to breaking point, the relatively new synthesis of evolutionary psychology – that branch of science that studies human psychology from a scientific, evolutionary standpoint – may offer a way, or at least the startings of a way, out of the mess we find ourselves in.

To return to my beginning, and to W. H. Auden. The task that lies ahead of us involves a rediscovery of connectivity, a continual exploration of the tension between what it means to be an individual and what it means to be a social being, a social being whose society is, increasingly, not just our immediate communities but the whole world.

To inform and direct that exploration requires a new moral framework, tough enough and flexible enough to bend with the winds of globalisation and global turmoil, a moral framework predicated on the organic, life-giving power of the human imagination. It sounds like a big idea, and it is. Heaven knows, now is not the time to be shrinking from big ideas. I myself have no answers to these questions, only glimmerings of suggestions. I expect few of you have answers either ... by yourselves. We can make a difference by helping each other to connect the dots of our individual experiences into a collective and continually evolving experience that could, given nurture and care, transform ourselves and our world.

The years ahead will require a great test of moral imagination.

VIEW FROM THE CHAIR

John Quinn

The Friday afternoon syndrome. I remember it so well from my teaching days. An air of lassitude and restlessness. 'Sir can we not play football? Have a debate? Read? Do anything but work?' Stolen glances at the classroom clock ...

I hoped it wouldn't be so this time, but even Céifin conferences have a wind-down aspect, and to be asked to chair the final session on Friday afternoon did give me a slight feeling of unease. Would the audience even stay around, or be tempted to leave early to avoid the Friday evening traffic? I felt even more uneasy as I had been indirectly responsible for the presence of both speakers.

An innovative piece of scheduling saved the day (nothing new at Céifin!). A father and son 'intergenerational discussion' on 'a framework for a new reality'. Intriguing prospect. That should solve the 'Friday afternoon syndrome'.

I knew the father well. John Abbott's ideas on education had prompted me to invite him to give the 2001 Open Mind Guest Lecture. It was very favourably received. I only met the son for the first time on Friday morning. Peter Abbott was a bright young man. Double First in English Literature at Cambridge, President of the Cambridge Union. Peter went in to bat first ...

A quote from Auden made us sit up – 'We must love one another or die'. No-one exists alone. Peter argued passionately for connectivity, not at a superficial level, but at a deep level. He made an interesting link between connection and imagination. Imagination he sees as the essence of compassion, the beginning of morality. The reason for our disconnectedness is a failure of morality, of moral imagination. We need a new moral framework based on imagination.

The 'old man' steps up to the crease and surveys the field. There is more than a glint of pride in his eye. Fatherly pride in a son who has acquitted himself well. Here is a father who hails the 'bloody mindedness of adolescence' – that beautiful time when we 'know everything, do everything, dare everything'.

The Abbott household must have been an interesting place some years ago. John Abbott's view of the process of education is an indictment of 'the measurable', the 'only one right answer' approach where by and large, teachers do what the government tells them to do. We are the learning species, Abbott senior argues. We must go with the grain of the brain. We are over-teaching and under-educating our young people. In a true spirit of subsidiarity we should 'let go' and recognise maturity in our schools.

Reminds me of some favourite lines from Seamus Heaney:

> Let go, let fly, forget
>> You've listened long enough
>> Now strike your note ...

Individually and collectively, father and son have struck their note. The framework for a new reality will foster confidence, creativity, curiosity, imagination.

Four p.m. Close of Conference. Not a sign of the Friday afternoon syndrome. Not one of the full-house audience wanted to play football. And I was the only one watching the clock. Well, a chairman has to do these things ...

CONFERENCE 2003

Global Aspirations/Local Reality
Are They Worlds Apart?

West County Conference & Leisure Centre,
Ennis,
County Clare
5th –7th November 2003

For further information please contact:
Máire Johnston, Conference Co-ordinator
Geraldine Kelly, Assistant Co-ordinator
The Céifin Centre
Town Hall, Shannon, Co.Clare
Tel 061-365912 /3   Fax 061-361954
Email ceifinconference@eircom.net
Website www.ceifin.com

'Romantic Ireland's dead and gone, it's with O'Leary in the grave', was the poet's cry a century ago. On the cusp of the third millennium many people fear the death of the Irish sense of community. The concept of a caring society seems well-buried in the selfishness of consumerism and mé-féinism encouraged by the phenomenon of the Celtic Tiger.

These were the concerns that inspired Fr Harry Bohan to organise a conference on the theme 'Are We Forgetting Something? Our Society in the New Millennium' in November 1998. Topics address ranged from the human search for meaning, to the economic boom in context.

This provocative and incisive volume, ably edited by Harry Bohan and Gerard Kennedy, also includes the views of the three chairpersons of the conference: Marie Martin, John Quinn and Michael Kenny, and is interspersed with well-chosen poetic and spiritual reflections on the topics addressed.

Are we forgetting something?

Are we forgetting something?

Our society in the new millennium

Edited by Harry Bohan & Gerard Kennedy

ISBN 1 85390 457 0

€11.45

ISBN 1 85390 474 0

€11.45

There is growing consensus that corporate and market values now shape Irish society.

Economic growth is synonymous with progress. But economic activity represents only one facet of human existence. Its values are not the only values that prevail in society. As we begin a new millennium, our society must be challenged to wonder what direction it is taking. There is an obvious need to ensure that the agenda of the corporate world and the welfare of local communities can co-exist in a meaningful relationship.

These are the concerns that were addressed at the 'Working Towards Balance' conference, organised by Rural Resource Development Ltd, the papers of which are published in this book.

Working Towards Balance

Redefining Roles and Relationships?

These annual conferences in Ennis are establishing themselves as an important date in the calendar and meeting a need for serious discussion about major social and ethical issues of the day.

Mary Robinson
United Nations High Commissioner for Human Rights

The papers presented at the Ennis Conference 2000 are collected in this book. The need to redine roles and relationships in a rapidly changing society was examined in many areas of modern life.

Papers include: 'Contemplating Alternative Relationships of Power in a Historical Perspective', Georóid Ó Tuathaigh; 'Rebuilding Social Capital: Restoring an Ethic of Care in Irish Society', Maureen Gaffney; 'Rise of Science, Rise of Atheism: Challenge to Christianity', Bill Collins; 'Social Justice and Equality in Ireland', Kathleen Lynch; 'Putting People at the Centre of things', Robert E. Lane; 'Why Are We Deaf to the Cry of the Earth?', Seán McDonagh; 'It's Just the Media', Colum Kenny

ISBN 1 85390 526 3

€11.45

Is The Future My Responsibility?

Have we become helpless in the face of change or can we manage the future? More and more people talk about the emptiness of modern life, they wonder where meaning is coming from and what values are shaping us; they say it is not easy being young today in spite of the choices and the freedom. We cannot assume that if we simply sit back and comment the storm will blow over, or that we will return to the old ways. The fact is we are experiencing a cultural transformation, we are witnessing the passing of a tradition, the end of an era. Every day we hear questions like 'Why aren't they doing something about it?' or 'Who is responsible for this, that or the other?' It is time to ask: 'Have I got any responsibility for the way things are?'

Including contributions from Nobel laureate John Hume and internationally renowned writer and broadcaster Charles Handy, *Is the Future My Responsibility?* is the fourth book of papers from the Céifin conference, held annually in Ennis, County Clare, and published by Veritas.

ISBN 1 85390 605 0   €12.50